EPOCHS OF
ITALIAN LITERATURE

EPOCHS

OF

ITALIAN LITERATURE

By

CESARE FOLIGNO *M.A.*

KENNIKAT PRESS
Port Washington, N. Y./London

EPOCHS OF ITALIAN LITERATURE

First published in 1920
Reissued in 1970 by Kennikat Press
Library of Congress Catalog Card No: 78-103223
SBN 8046-0860-1

Manufactured by Taylor Publishing Company   Dallas, Texas

CONTENTS

PAGE

THE DAWN 7

THE RENAISSANCE 17

THE TRANSITION TO MODERN TIMES 31

THE RISE OF THE NATION . . . 39

MODERN ITALY 57

List of Authors and their Works 73

Alphabetical Index of Authors 89

☞ The stress accent is indicated by ˋ in all Italian words in which the stressed syllable is not the penultimate. It is placed also on certain penultimate syllables which might by mispronunciation be made antipenultimate.

No discrimination is made between open and close vowels.

The   D A W N

ITALIAN was not, among Romance languages, the first to claim the dignity of a literary language. Italians realized but late that, even though Latin was still considered the literary language of the country lying between the Alps and the sea, there was room for a new literary language that should share with it the field of science and literature, with claims not inferior to those which French or Provençal could urge in France. The spoken language of Italy, the vernacular, during the ten centuries that separate Augustus from King Arduin, had diverged more and more from the recognized language of science and art, literary Latin; and, while learned writers laboured for a couple of centuries longer under the delusion that they were full heirs to the perfect craftsmanship of Cicero and Horace, the distinction between the vernacular (*volgare*) and the literary language (*lingua di grammàtica*) was becoming evident to all. Nor, under the improving social conditions, was it possible to debar from all literary enjoyment those who were ignorant of Latin, any more than it was practicable for judges to continue the use of Latin in the courts, when those who appeared before them understood nothing but the vernacular.

The peoples of France and Spain, being farther removed from Rome, were faced by difficulties similar but less formidable. Among them Roman tradition was less active. Few, if any, of the inhabitants of Gaul or Iberia regarded themselves as the descendants of the Romans.

Italians, on the other hand, were never troubled with a doubt in the matter. And yet traders penned their crude business letters in the vernacular, and country swains, on the slopes of the Alps or in the cloudless Sicilian moonlights, endeavoured to win their loves, like the nightingale or the thrush, with singing; and their songs were in the vernacular.

The spoken language, developing in cities and regions often isolated by scant facilities for traffic, acquired dialectal peculiarities : but the continued presence of the parent language prevented a dialect, and especially a dialect of a neighbouring region, from becoming incomprehensible to those who spoke a different one, and gradually, as social conditions improved and communication became easier, a process of levelling towards uniformity set in.

The earliest writings in vernacular Italian are dialectal : pious songs, moral admonitions, translations of religious works from the Latin, renderings of French epics. Among them is, for instance, the *Laudes Creaturarum* by St. Francis of Assisi ; many an Umbrian peculiarity occurs also in the *Laude* of Fra Jacopone da Todi, so rich in sincere feeling, which were written at the end of the thirteenth century ; a strong Sicilian coating covers the *contrasto* by Cielo Dàlcamo ; and dialectal features mark other poems of the same century,—poems of love, of war, and politics. During the first half of the century Frederick II of Hohenstaufen, the son of a Norman queen, had vainly endeavoured to suppress under his stern imperial rule the ambitions of many cities and communes for local freedom. A new spirit was permeating the peninsula ; trade had brought wealth to many, and with it a new consciousness of rights. Gradually the not numerous Germanic settlers (Lombards, Franks, Goths, and Saxons) who had kept aloof from town life, and had attempted to dominate the country without mixing with the people, were forced by the town-dwellers, who were mainly of Latin stock, to yield some of their privileges, to abandon their country castles, and to live in towns, where their wealth, drawn from landed estates, was overshadowed by the newly acquired and increasing riches of business men. After long struggles the towns celebrated their victories by the erection of churches and town halls; and soon master craftsmen—sculptors, painters, and architects—gave evidence of a fresh artistic impulse not entirely independent of classical traditions.

Literature could no longer keep silent. At the court of Frederick II, ever rushing from one end of Italy to the other, ever crowded by noblemen and statesmen of different regions, some writers, encouraged by the emperor himself, attempted vernacular imitations of Provençal troubadours. The language used by these writers—men of good taste and much travelled—was free from the more pronounced dialectal forms and approximated unconsciously to the vernacular forms that appeared less remote from Latin. Both style and thought came from France. In the footsteps of these 'Sicilian' poets (as they are wrongly called) followed several writers in central Italy who used what was practically the Tuscan vernacular; they were often more sincere, more learned, and more gifted than their predecessors. Their art reached its highest development in the lyrics of Guido Guinizelli of Bologna and Guido Cavalcanti the Florentine. Italian poetical style was formed.

Nor did prose lag behind. In that wonderful dawn of Italian art many set themselves the task of translating learned works from Latin and French, chiefly moral treatises, allegorical poems, Arthurian romances, or folk-tales. Prose style being naturally influenced by its various models, Italian syntax was mainly cast in a Latin mould, as appears in such writings as *Il Novellino* and the *Conti di antichi cavalieri*.

When, in 1283, Dante Alighieri at the age of eighteen wrote his first sonnet, it was clear that the Tuscan vernacular was to become the literary language of Italy. His own successful use of it won for it ultimate pre-eminence over all claimants, even though in an unfinished Latin work (*De vulgari eloquentia*) he urged the choice of the best elements of each dialect as the only way to form a sound and living Italian vernacular. The loosely-knit prose of his *Vita nuova* (1292) has a peculiarly tender effectiveness; more Latin and more complex in its syntax is the prose of his *Convivio* (1308). The lyrical and allegorical poems contained in these two works soon gained for him great fame; and when after his death (1321) his poem, *La Commèdia*, at which he had been working for many a year, became known in its completeness in literary circles, all discussion ceased. Yet he himself and his contemporaries were under the impression that Latin was still a living language in Italy.

Dante's lyrics are more fully appreciated when they are placed in their natural setting. A philosophical theory of love had been evolved by Guinizelli at Bologna, and its influence is seen in his own verses and in those of Cavalcanti. The latter had been almost the centre of a Florentine group of poets of *stil nuovo*, as they called themselves, to which Dante belonged, together with Lapo Gianni, Dino Frescobaldi, and others. Cino de' Sigisbuldi of Pistòia, the learned lawyer, was at one and the same time the friend of Dante, the last of the poets of *stil nuovo,* and the link between this group and Petrarch. These all aimed at great polish. A less cultured vein was represented, at this time, by the irrepressible wastrel, Cecco Angiolieri, as it had been a few years earlier by Ciacco dell' Anguillàia.

From the first half of the fourteenth century we are able to probe every side of Italian life through literary works of the time. Thus, in his *Del reggimento e costume di donna,* Francesco da Barberino tells how women ought to be educated and ought to behave, and in the *Documenti d'amore* he has given us precepts about morals, wisdom, and courtesy. From the *Fioretti di San Francesco* we gain an insight into the Franciscan atmosphere that enveloped so many in Tuscany at the time; and even though we may have little time to spend upon the pious works of Domenico Cavalca, we may linger to admire the clear-cut and robust style of his brother Dominican, Bartolomeo da San Concòrdio, who collected wise sayings of ancient and mediaeval writers in his *Ammaestramenti degli antichi.* Dino Compagni's admirable little *Crònica,* so honest and forcible, helps us to understand the political difficulties against which Dante and his fellow-citizens struggled ; while a glance at some parts of the chronicle written by Giovanni Villani, himself a merchant, will show how wide and far-reaching the outlook was among the business men of Florence and how important the part played by Florentine bankers in European politics.

Meanwhile Latin was not set aside. Some men had striven to improve upon the style of their predecessors, but the chief promoter of the revival of classical learning was Francesco Petrarca. Monuments and statues of

Greece and Rome were being brought to light; Petrarch spent his best energies in discovering classical manuscripts; many forgotten works were by him and through him and his followers restored to scholars; many more were purged of the mistakes of ignorant scribes. Petrarch was bent upon reviving the study of Latin, and succeeded in reviving it, but, as an unexpected result, it became evident that Latin was no longer a living language since scholarly mediaeval works seemed to be almost a caricature of classical Latin. And thus finally Italians discovered that their sole language was the vernacular, though for a long time to come they were not conscious of the ultimate results of their efforts. Thus we find that Petrarch himself, who composed many poetical and prose works in the language of the Romans, affected to consider his Italian poems, the *Canzoniere* and the *Trionfi*, as mere trifles. Born at Arezzo in Tuscany (1304), he naturally wrote in Tuscan, and his example, following upon Dante's, and strengthened by that of his friend Giovanni Boccàccio, the author of the *Decamerón*, finally established the Tuscan vernacular as the literary language. Discussions about the language of Italy were to arise again during the later Renaissance period, and to be rife once more in the days of Manzoni, but the question was settled for all practical purposes by the great triumvirate of the fourteenth century.

The birth of Italian entailed the death of the mother language. It was long before Italians, who had been accustomed to consider themselves the owners of the untold riches of Roman literature and history, could bring themselves to renounce such assets and to abide by their newly discovered poverty—a promising poverty, however, which allowed great hopes of future development to be entertained, but which threw the Italians into a difficult world, into the struggle for pre-eminence, and required from them unexpected and untiring efforts. They were given a language that had no past; it rested with them to breathe into it a new spirit. They were to express the story of their dreams, their aspirations, their thoughts, their sufferings and joys, in the mellow and silvery sounds of a virgin language.

By the end of the fourteenth century the literary language was established. If the language was new, the people were politically old. They were cursed by the consequences of sins not their own ; the very privilege of having been born in the country from which Rome had ruled the world, and where one of the great powers of the Middle Ages had its seat, was the cause of untold suffering. The wonderful beauty of nature in the peninsula was by turns a remedy for this suffering and an addition to it.

Latin was still the language of culture ; culture was still universal, not national, in character. This fact, which was not without effect in other countries at the time, hindered the natural development of Italian literature. The inextricable confusion in political conditions conspired to the same result.

A river sometimes separates into two branches to unite again later. So Italian literature had at its beginnings two branches, one Italian and the other Latin. It is the custom to read only the Italian works, but we ought to bear in mind that, in doing so, we overlook a great part of the literary activity of the time. It was in Latin that Dante himself wrote his epistles, two eclogues, and the treatises *De monarchia* and *De vulgari eloquentia* ; and it is in such works as his *Secretum, De vita solitaria, De ocio religiosorum, De remediis utriusque fortunae, Itinera-rium Syriacum*, and especially in his numerous letters, that Petrarch's individuality is most clearly apparent. Indeed, his letters, even in the Italian translation by Fracassetti, must be known to all who wish to see more than one side of his mind.

It is otherwise with Boccàccio ; it is in his Italian works that he reveals himself to us ; his Latin works do not add much to our knowledge of him. In the *Decameròn* he appears as a zestful teller of stories ; in the *Fiammetta*, a prose novel, he allows much of his own joys and griefs to transpire ; even his poem *Filòstrato* is not devoid of autobiographical interest. In *Ameto* he gave us the most ancient Italian bucolic, and in the *Ninfale fiesolano* a short and charming mythologic and idyllic poem.

Dante, Petrarch, and Boccàccio entirely dominate their age. Petrarch in the *Trionfi*, and Boccàccio in the *Amorosa visione*, were influenced by the *Commèdia*, but in general that masterpiece discouraged imitation, and writers who attempted it, such as Fàzio degli Uberti and Federico Frezzi, met with little success.

Lyric slowly passed from the imitation of the poets of *stil nuovo* and of Dante, as in Matteo Frescobaldi and in Giovanni Quirini, to the imitation of Petrarch, as in Cino Rinuccini and Buonaccorso da Montemagno. Among all these, and others unnamed here, Quirini has the strongest and most gifted personality.

Story-telling has long been a popular pastime. There are in Boccàccio's *Decameròn* stories that had been told many centuries before in India and in Persia, that had been retold in mediaeval France, and that, with the inevitable modifications, may be traced down to modern novels or short stories. The human imagination does not seem to command a great variety of fundamental schemes for a tale. Ser Giovanni Fiorentino and Giovanni Sercambi will not therefore be criticized so much on account of their imitations as for the coldness and coarseness which they respectively evinced in their works, whereas spirited Franco Sacchetti told his stories in a familiar and artless style, so near to the spoken language that they are pleasing to this day, the more so because in his three hundred *Novelle* he has given us anecdotes of his contemporaries.

Boccàccio had taken many of his subjects from common life, but had clothed them in an elegant style ; Sacchetti kept nearer to the popular level both in his prose and his verse ; and he, together with Pieràccio Tebaldi, Antònio Pucci, and a few lesser writers, form a group of poets who sang for the Florentine middle class about Florence, about Florentine women, popular heroes, vices and virtues, country amusements, and historical events. In Siena Bindo Bònichi, and in Ferrara Antònio Beccari, belonged to the same class of poets, the latter allowing his restless and wayward spirit to find full expression in his verses.

In this first flush of Italian literature there was no real epic and no drama. There were poems on historical subjects, but they were *serventesi* or *lamenti*. The former were in a metre that by the frequent repetition of the rhyme allowed the singer to gain an easy hearing from the crowds to whom it expounded, in its own fashion, contemporary events. The latter were the natural outcome of political conditions : wars were continuous ; the smaller communes were slowly compelled to accept the rule of the larger towns ; petty tyrants, the more cruel and suspicious because of their weakness, appeared in many cities and often ended their meteoric careers at the hand of political foes. And the poets, echoing popular feeling, or sometimes wishing to influence it, impersonated in these *lamenti* the defeated, the decimated, or the famishing towns, and bewailed their woes. But such songs were not epics; no more were the sonnets by which Francesco di Vannozzo encouraged Giàn Galeazzo Visconti, lord of Lombardy, to unite the whole of Italy under his sway. There could be no epic, because Italian history did not provide the necessary subject. Heroes of the French *chansons de gestes* became popular in Italy, and were sung in artless poems for the mere pleasure of the hearers,—since no national glory, no pride or sorrow, moved the poet or his audience. Often the paladins of Charlemagne acquired the features of Arthurian knights. The mingling of those two great poetic cycles began in Italy at an early date; the names of Roland, Charlemagne, Tristan, and Lancelot became equally familiar, and, while the courtly and more cultured preferred the adventures of the Knights of the Round Table, as did Pàolo and Francesca, the less cultured listened with greater pleasure to songs wherein the rougher paladins of Charlemagne wielded unfailing swords among hordes of Saracens. To this day the people of certain provinces read and sing of them with unabated interest. But those were but echoes of epics, not material whence real epic could spring; especially among a people that was no less foreign in race than in feeling. A heroic background is necessary to epic and to drama, and there was lacking in mediaeval Italy continuity of political effort centred in national heroes great and famous enough to give rise to them.

The Renaissance

TREADING in Petrarch's steps cultured Italians during the fifteenth and the sixteenth centuries came into direct contact with the greatest works of ancient Rome. They were able to appreciate them correctly, though with the enthusiam of neophytes they were inclined to overrate them. As the most gifted minds of the time were drawn into this movement, the vernacular literature was impoverished, and the literature of the country became in great part independent of the people and incomprehensible to them.

Had political conditions been different, such an event could not have occurred. The northern and central cities, in their struggle for independence and for supremacy, had exhausted their energies ; social conflict had already sapped them ; local parties had mostly a social and economic basis : there resulted frequent revolutions and excesses, and their natural issue, reaction. The innate yearning after peace and security easily overcame all other considerations in the exhausted minds of the citizens, and even those communes that had longest preserved their republican form fell by degrees, in fact, if not always in name, into the power of tyrants.

With the exception of Venice, where a stern oligarchy had prevented social upheavals and forestalled a tyranny, the principal cities in Italy at the beginning of the fifteenth century were ruled by tyrants, in Naples a king, in most of the other states *Signori* of feudal, military, or commercial origin. These states sometimes contended with each other, rarely for economic advantages, but for the most part because the *Signori* (Machiavelli called them *Principi*), feeling their own weakness, hoped to remedy it by enlarging their domain. By adopting an ever-favoured prescription they endeavoured to divert the attention of their subjects from internal to foreign politics. Yet the shrewd people of Italy allowed themselves to be deceived only in part. They refused to consider such wars their own business, and this was not the least of the causes that provoked the adoption of mercenary troops.

Thus we find in Italy many princely courts, the pope's among them, more or less estranged from their subjects, defended by mercenary troops, and thronged with mercenary literary men and mercenary artists. The *Signore* pursued a logical policy. The people had to be impressed by the splendour of his court in order to strengthen his authority. All orders for buildings and paintings and statues were in his gift ; and even writers, whether poets or classical scholars, were, with few exceptions, in need of princely patronage. As a consequence they swarmed to the courts, as teachers of the noble heirs of the princes, as diplomats, or as courtiers, and the more willingly since the classical revival had inspired its devotees with an unquenchable thirst for glory. They gradually gained such an influence as to convince some of the *Signori* that the one great aim of a ruler should be the furthering of art and the protection of its ministers. Thus all values were altered. So we may explain the conduct of princes like Lorenzo de' Mèdici, Lodovico Sforza, Isabella d'Este, and Leo X, some of whom deserve indeed great praise for their untiring efforts in furthering learning and art.

Among the mercenary troops there were splendid soldiers and many capable and even great leaders ; and the world may see to this day to what height of perfection the artists and the writers of the Italian Renaissance attained. But soldiers, painters, and poets had lost contact with their fellows and the world outside. Bernardino Luini was calmly painting one of his most beautiful madonnas not far from Pavia while the great battle between the troops of Charles V and of Francis I was being fought.

Poets and men of letters seeing freedom lost and the unity of Italy impossible, seeing the country overrun and pillaged by foreign troops, seeing the people listless or absorbed in the gorgeous pageants provided by the *Signori*, were driven to seek refuge in the cold pleasures of exact scholarship or in the polish of stylistic form. And because of this estrangement between the realities of life and the writers who ought to have given those realities their artistic expression, Italian literature may be said for the time to have lost its soul.

A number of classical scholars and researchers had full sway at the outset : Pòggio Bracciolini, Niccolò Nìccoli, Leonardo Bruni, Ambrògio Traversari, discovered manuscripts, formed large collections of the classics, studied, annotated, and interpreted them. Francesco Filelfo was among the first to have a real knowledge of Greek ; Gasparino Barzizza and Guarino of Verona spread the study of Latin among their young pupils ; Vittorino da Feltre opened a famous school on new and efficient principles of education ; Pope Niccolò V (Tomaso Parentucelli) favoured classical learning, and Pope Pius II (Enea Sìlvio Piccolòmini) was among the leading scholars of his age ; Lorenzo Valla brought a modern spirit of criticism to bear upon literary and historical problems; archaeological studies were initiated by Flàvio Biondo and Cirìaco de' Pizzicolli ; Gioviano Pontano and Politian (Àngelo

Ambrogini) wrote poems in Latin and Greek so perfect in form as to be worthy of the ancients, and yet infused a modern spirit into them; platonic theories were revived in Florence, and Marsìlio Ficino, Cristòforo Landino, and Pico della Miràndola became their greatest exponents.

Few works were written in Italian under the absolute rule of classicism, and of those the majority were strictly conformed to ancient models and lacking in inspiration. We must look to the Florentine barber Burchiello's burlesque verses and to those of the Venetian scholar Leonardo Giustiniàn to find sincere inspiration before the middle of the fifteenth century. Lorenzo de' Mèdici (1449–92), being widely read in old Italian poetry and himself a poet, set the example of writing again in Italian. He composed idylls (*Ambra*), parodies, poems of peasant life (*Nència da Barberino*), platonic love poems, and coarse if spirited carnival songs. Politian followed in his steps, and being endowed with a rare poetic faculty, succeeded in making his simple songs, his *canti carnascialeschi*, and his occasional poems, such as the *Stanze per la giostra*, into real works of art. In the cities, especially in Florence, in Rome, in Ferrara, literature became at the end of the fifteenth century a popular pastime favoured by the middle classes and by tradesmen, no less than by the courts. Cleverly constructed lyrics made a strong appeal to the refined taste of dwellers in towns who had become enthusiastic *dilettanti*. Instead of the poets finding fresh inspiration in the opinions and sentiments of the people, the latter sought refuge from everyday humdrum life in the works of skilled craftsmen of verse; hence formal perfection wedded to frigid repetition of timeworn motives characterizes the countless lyrics of Bernardo Accolti, Antònio Tebaldeo, Serafino Aquilano, and to some extent even those of Cariteo. Alone among lyric writers, Matteo Maria Boiardo, who sang of a personal love, and on account of his position and character was independent of popular fashion, could write a *canzoniere* of real beauty.

In fact lyrical poetry can be attractive only when it is inspired by sincere passion, and the men of the Renaissance had assumed towards life a detached attitude that was bound to wither inspiration. Even a man like Cardinal Pietro Bembo (1470–1547), who accepted the new platonic theories of the Florentine group, composed a *canzoniere* that is, indeed, free from the faults to be found in some of the intervening poets, but is interesting only as an able imitation of Petrarch. Bembo acquired an extraordinary domination over his contemporaries. Petrarch was imitated henceforward through the medium of Bembo, and few writers, with his arguments (*Prose della volgàr lingua*) and example before them, thought of Italian as being independent of Petrarch and the Tuscan dialect.

Bembo swept away by his example all improvised and courtly-mannered verse. A painstaking imitation of Petrarch's motives and language became the rule. The lyrics of Àngelo di Costanzo, Galeazzo di Tàrsia, Luigi Tansillo, and Bernardino Rota would seldom meet with favour from a modern reader ; and the poems of women writers are scarcely better than elegant literary exercises, such as the lyrics of Vittòria Colonna, Verònica Gàmbara, Tùllia d'Aragona, Verònica Franco, and others ; only Gàspara Stampa, in her songs of a real love, struck a sincere and effective note.

Torquato Tasso, who flourished near the end of the sixteenth century, found in his own melancholy the inspiration of his songs, which, though reminiscent of the fashionable Petrarchism, were not unworthy of his extraordinary poetic talent. And Michelàngelo stands prominent among the multitude by reason of the originality of his lyrical poetry. His devotion to Vittòria Colonna was sincere. Moreover, he was, as real genius nearly always is, in advance of his contemporaries. His mind and his art were not content with the mere imitation of beauty. The tragedy of the time was apparent to him and is articulate in all his works. If we seek a representative of this age, it is to Michelàngelo that we must look, as the giant summing up in himself and dominating the Renaissance ; but in him we have also a premonition of the future.

Count Matteo Maria Boiardo (1434-94) is an interesting figure ; a rich and respected nobleman and statesman, he sought relaxation from political labours in literature, and wrote Latin eclogues, translations from the Latin and Greek, and poems of love ; and as he belonged to a noble family and was proud of it, he felt in sympathy with the world of chivalry.

Luigi Pulci (1432-84) in his *Morgante* had given literary form to rude popular poems about Charlemagne's paladins ; Boiardo aimed higher ; he surrounded his *Orlando innamorato* with Arthurian and Carolingian knights, and he enjoyed living with them in his fancy and singing their noble exploits, though sometimes a smile gathered to his lips as he remembered that after all these things belonged to an era that was past.

Since the thirteenth century knights and ladies had been eager readers of Arthurian poems. The place filled by novels in modern literature was held by such romantic poems and by *novelle*, but these, being written in prose, lacked the enchanting lilt of mellow verse. Boiardo himself was a devotee of this kind of literature, and in his turn guided his readers through distant ages, dark forests, joyous feasts, gorgeous tournaments, heroic fights against the heathen and against monsters.

Lodovico Ariosto (1474–1533), a far greater artist, laboured with untiring care on *Orlando furioso*. Probably his heart was not so fully captivated by his subject as Boiardo's had been. He wished to indulge the taste of his public and to entertain them, and therefore he conceived a chevaleresque poem, and because he lived at a time when the feeling for beauty among the cultured had acquired a passionate intensity, he lavished upon his poem all the adornments of which his fertile genius and his consummate craftsmanship were capable. His attitude towards chivalry is similar to Raphael's attitude towards religion. Most of Raphael's paintings have religious subjects, and yet religion had certainly not a primary place in his mind. His saints and madonnas are to him just what chevaleresque knights and adventurers are to Ariosto, the means of giving expression to the beautiful. Both are unsurpassable artists, but both are artists of a period in which art, while it influenced life, did not have its roots in it.

The success of the *Furioso* was such that imitations swarmed like flies on a summer day and were as annoying. Against such pests were aimed Aretino's parody *Orlandino* and Folengo's *Baldus*, the masterpiece of macaronic poetry.

In an age steeped in classical learning the success of the *Furioso*, disregarding as it did all that Aristotle had said about epic, could not but prompt a reactionary return to

regular epic. Attempts such as the epic poems by
Trissino, Alamanni, and Bernardo Tasso, pointed to a
tendency which at a later period through the genius of
Torquato Tasso brought its natural fruit (1544–95) in
the *Gerusalemme liberata*, a poem as observant of the
unities as the taste of the time would allow; a poem, moreover, centred in a religious subject in strict accordance with
the hard-and-fast principles of the counter-reformation.
Tasso had in his youth taken a first step in this direction
with his *Rinaldo*, and later he submitted the *Liberata* to
the judgement of pious and learned critics, and revised it
with a view to the avoidance of heterodoxy; the product of
much painstaking effort was the *Gerusalemme conquistata*,
a poem inferior to the *Liberata*.

We may class as akin to epic a number of poems
on religious themes, among which Tansillo's *Le Làgrime
di San Pietro* and Tasso's *Le Sette giornate del mondo
creato* are the most celebrated.

Life even at princely courts showed jarring contrasts
of extreme refinement and coarse brutality; the less
cultured classes lacked the refinement, but all shared in
a corruption that was the outcome of general causes.
The spirit of freedom and independence was gradually
extinguished by the habit of subjection to local tyrants,
however able, art-loving, and learned, and by the
hopelessness of rebellion. Thus was the way paved for
foreign domination. The South was being steadily
accustomed to it. In rapid succession, between 1494 and
1509, the armies of France, of Spain, and of the emperor
overran Italy, nor was the country to be rid of them for
centuries to come. Between 1527 and 1530 Rome was
sacked and Florence besieged and crushed. Only in
Florence, where the spirit of a new age mingled its flame

with the last flicker of a glorious tradition, was resistance shown. Savonarola's preaching had produced an outburst of mediaeval puritanism and of communal pride ; Rome's fate was taken as a symbol of the sufferings that were to be imposed upon Italy, and caused in Florence a sudden ferment of patriotic heroism. Michelàngelo, who had shown himself alive to feelings that only in later years would become general, was among its defenders.

Religious feeling was waning, even though the outward cult was rarely abandoned ; pagan classicism had shaken the foundations of belief among the learned, few of whom were affected by the revival of platonism ; the pursuit of pleasure had deadened the capacity for spiritual emotion ; the mundane corruption of the clergy arose from similar causes and alienated the religious affections of the people ; art enwrapped the teachings of Christianity in a golden mist of sensuous beauty.

Popes, more imbued with heathen learning than with piety, or burning with political passion rather than religion, failed to inspire zeal for the faith in their flock. The artificial revival of ancient and heathen ideals and conceptions, isolated attempts to rekindle the fire of religion, isolated examples of Christian piety or of stoic virtue, the spread of platonic idealism—none of these could exert a profound influence. The Renaissance with its glamour was to disappear when the counter-reformation movement took Italy in its grip. Tasso experienced the torment of the dying Renaissance, of the reawakened religious zeal, and of the birth of a new era. He lived when the star of the Renaissance was setting. While it was rising, society was pervaded by corruption, and writers of *novelle* drew a minute picture of social conditions and customs. No less than

Boiardo and Ariosto, they aimed at entertaining their readers, though by means less ambitious. Boccàccio had set an example that invited imitation, and his imitators chose their subjects and their background each according to his own predilection. Sermini and Fortiṇi are artless and coarse, Sabbadino degli Arienti, Parabosco, Giraldi and Erizzo dull. Masùccio Salernitano denounces the immorality about which he writes. Among these many writers of *novelle* stands out the name of Matteo Bandello (1480–1565), whose work, though lacking vivacity, is an inexhaustible source of information about the life at the Italian courts in the sixteenth century. Machiavelli, Àgnolo Firenzuola, and Antonfrancesco Doni also wrote *novelle*, and to theirs may be added one by Luigi da Porto (1485–1529), *Giulietta e Romeo*, and a score, very spirited, by Antonfrancesco Grazzini, il Lasca (1503–84). Such works enjoyed great favour in social and literary circles.

In an age athirst for amusement the drama had naturally a great vogue. Mystery plays had been frequently represented in Tuscany throughout the fifteenth century; Politian was the first who attempted with his *Orfeo* (1471) a play in vernacular on a non-religious subject. Soon afterwards at the court of Ferrara comedies by Plautus and Terence in Italian translations were staged with great pomp, and it was on these that the comedies of Ariosto were modelled,— vivacious and witty, but none the less faithful to the Roman design. After him, comedies came to be written in increasing numbers ; Cardinal Dovizi sought to infuse new interest into an ancient subject by portraying contemporary characters, and Machiavelli, borrowing the theme from his age, assimilated the *commedia* to the *novella* (*Mandràgola*), thus giving to his work a fresh and satirical effectiveness. His example bore fruit in the fact that practically all the subjects of tales were dramatized in course of time. There are plays of different merit by Lorenzino de' Mèdici, Francesco d'Ambra, Lasca, Giovàn Maria Cecchi, Annibal Caro, Pietro Aretino, and, later, Giordano Bruno. Yet theatres were a privilege of the courts, and the populace preferred the simple and coarse farces that had developed from the mystery plays. These were sometimes written out in full, but, when their numbers grew and professional companies began to be formed, only their plot (*scenàrio*) was written out, the dialogue being improvised by experienced actors whose sallies and antics formed the principal attraction. Thus arose the *commèdia dell' arte*, which steadily gained favour with the audiences, was imitated by foreign writers no less than the regular comedy, and in the eighteenth century was the subject of Goldoni's reform.

The peculiar conditions of the age were rather inclined to comedy than to tragedy. Beauty and art were sought after because they helped to veil the tragic misery of a people split up into small states, overridden by foreign armies, plundered and bereft of hope. Nevertheless tragedies were written by Trìssino, Giraldi, Speroni, Luigi Groto, and Tasso, some following the model of Seneca, others that of Greek plays; but the spirit was lacking and these attempts fell flat and remained barren. Pastoral drama secured a far greater success. Boccàccio had written a pastoral novel, which Jàcopo Sannazzaro (1458–1530) imitated in the *Arcàdia*. Politian had composed a mythological drama, *Orfeo*, which had many imitators until Agostino Beccari brought out at Ferrara in 1554 his *Sacrifiziо*, the first real pastoral

drama, soon, however, to be overshadowed by Tasso's
Aminta (1573), simple, musical, and charming, and by
Guarini's *Pastòr Fido* (1590).

The Italian Renaissance refused to be lectured on
morals. Under the direct influence of Juvenal, Antònio
Vinciguerra composed his serious satires, but it is not
long before we find, in Ariosto, a change of tone. The
shafts he throws in his *Sàtire* are piercing at times, but
he seems resigned and almost reconciled to the hopelessness of his task. He draws a realistic picture of some
aspects of social life, he proclaims his desire to retire from
a disagreeable world, but does not dare to hope for an
improvement ; Tansillo and Lodovico Paterno were
equally without hope.

Francesco Berni (1497–1535), rather burlesque than
satirical, turned Ariosto's scholarly smile into cynical
laughter. Vices and failings were for him in his *capìtoli*
the subject of ridicule or jest and nothing more ; and
Lasca's satirical verse had only personal vengeance for
its aim.

The humanists had often attacked each other with
violent invective; literary quarrels were frequent and
bitter throughout the Renaissance. Caro and Castelvetro,
no less than Aretino and Niccolò Franco, used in their
rhymes all manner of missiles, the least seemly for choice.
Aretino excelled in anonymous epigrams and political
squibs against the papal government. They were hung
up under a statue called Pasquino in Rome, and were
consequently known as *Pasquinate* : they have given their
name to a literary genus.

If morals were banned, manners were worshipped.
Towards the middle of the fifteenth century, Leòn
Battista Alberti wrote his didactic treatise *Della*

famìglia; in 1528 Baldesàr Castiglione completed his code of the perfect courtier, *Il Cortegiano*, and in 1558 there appeared Della Casa's *Galateo*. Good manners were decorous and befitting for learned and polished courtiers, who enjoyed an immoral play and admired with the sensitiveness of the true artist a painting or a statue, who were prone to unruly passions and ready to discuss platonic love. Such contrasts can be paralleled in the lives of the artists also. Giòrgio Vasari, in his *Vite*, has left us precious accounts of them, and Benvenuto Cellini (1500–71), with unsophisticated sincerity, has given us a glimpse of sixteenth-century *vie de Bohême*; Machiavelli himself has told us how he could divide his day between unseemly escapades, games at cards in an inn, brawls with country yokels, and deep meditation and study.

Like Ariosto in the realm of pure poetry, Castiglione among courtiers, and Cellini among artists, Machiavelli (1469–1527) may claim to be a true exponent of his time among historians and students of politics. He was a dreamer of political dreams, an idealist, as Guicciardini pointed out; the greatness of Rome impressed him almost as much as it had bewitched Cola di Rienzo in the middle of the fourteenth century. He saw the tragic conditions of the Italy of his day; he could perceive no remedy except by a miracle; he had tried to work a miracle himself by forming a conscript army in Florence, and he had failed; he had almost seen a miracle performed by Caesar Bòrgia, who seemed to be on the way to unite Italy under his rule; he saw Ferdinand of Aragon highly successful in Spain and Italy, though as devoid of political morals as Caesar Bòrgia himself. He saw that morals played but a small part in contemporary life, and he attempted to awaken the Italians from their political indifference and hopelessness. In this he was a pioneer, but in this alone. It is because his ideas and ideals are presented with artistic realism in his writings that he became a byword of immorality. His *Prìncipe* may be said to be a portrait of the same Caesar Bòrgia that looks down upon us from many paintings, a striking personality. His *Discorsi* are a political treatise, and even his historical works are tinged by his theory of statecraft. A greater artist than he was a politician, he wrote the finest Italian prose of the Renaissance. Machiavelli saw that a new era was approaching and thought that the star of intellect and logic could lead Italy through the troubled seas.

While Machiavelli is ever swayed by political or artistic emotions, his friend Francesco Guicciardini (1483–1540) is cold, clear-sighted, practical. Machiavelli, burning with patriotic fervour, parades the immorality of some of his tenets; Guicciardini calmly ignores the existence of morals. He criticized one of Machiavelli's works in his *Considerazioni*, and his histories of Italy and of Florence are written with great care and considerable insight.

The Transition to Modern Times

THE period following upon the later Renaissance has been often misunderstood. Raphael and Ariosto represent the perfection of the Renaissance, the conquest of beauty and complete satisfaction in its enjoyment. They belong entirely to their age. But for Machiavelli there was no such satisfaction ; he tried to find the key to the future in the cult of the intellect. Leonardo da Vinci (1452–1519) strove to express intellectual emotions in his works, and was troubled by an infinite variety of scientific problems, for he believed that only through the knowledge and interpretation of nature could progress be attained. Tasso, again, suffered perpetual agony of mind by reason of the conflict between his idyllic and lyrical tendencies and the reactionary trend of the later sixteenth century. All their sufferings and attempts are concentrated in the solitary genius of Michelàngelo (1475–1564). In him the quest for beauty was the uplifting of the soul towards God. Religious-minded and an adherent of neo-platonism, he subjected the violent forces of nature to his idealism. In him there is no detachment. Art is life, and springs from nature and thought, not from learning. Neither was there detachment in Tasso or in Leonardo or in Machiavelli. While Tasso desired to be under the sway of beauty alone, as the men who had come before him, while Leonardo found satisfaction in nature, and Machiavelli in learning and the cult of intellect, Michelàngelo felt with instinctive insight the tragedy of his own age and of the age to come ; that is why he towers above his contemporaries as a great man and points the way to further developments.

Let us consider what had happened. Art had exhausted its possibilities as a means of expressing beauty.
Some northern peoples had cut adrift from the Church
of Rome, striking out for a more evangelical religion,
and for purer manners; while Rome after the Council of
Trent endeavoured to attain the same effects by reaction
and discipline. France and Spain had ceased since 1559
to fight for the possession of Italy, and the whole of the
country was dominated by the foreigner, with the sole
exceptions of Piedmont and Venice. Italy, in which,
during the Middle Ages, each town had been ablaze with
the love of liberty, had lost internal freedom during the
Renaissance through the establishment of the *Signori*;
now it had lost its national independence. Venice alone
continued the struggle in the near East, and the Dukes
of Savoy fought to keep and to enlarge their little state,
wedged in between France and the possessions of Spain.

Thought was no longer independent, because the
Council of Trent had sternly limited all freedom of
research within the compass of the defined dogmas; art
was no longer independent, because the glamour of the
Renaissance compelled to imitation; even manners were
no longer Italian—Spanish pomp and formality were
creeping into them. And yet the germs sown by
Machiavelli, by Michelàngelo, by Giordano Bruno, the
rebel monk, could not but be fruitful; in them at least
political independence was not entirely a memory of the
past.

The seventeenth century is often called a period of
stagnation in literature; it is rather a period of change
and of preparation. Literary men as well as artists felt
the necessity of some fundamental change, since improvement on the lines followed by the Renaissance masters

seemed to all impossible. Literature is now divided into two sections—the purely artistic and the scientific. Machiavelli, Leonardo, and Giordano Bruno had already shown such a partition to be necessary. Artists and writers who merely followed the lines of tradition, conscious of the necessity of some change yet devoid of individuality, fell into exaggerating such refinements as they found in the older masters. They never tried to commune with nature or to listen to the suggestions of their hearts. In fact it became a dogma to study the Renaissance masters rather than nature. Thence came the tedious habit of conceits and cold witticism ; verbosity and bombast were added after the example of Spain. Spanish influence had made itself felt in Naples as early as the fifteenth century, and the manners of the Neapolitans had been a subject of jest for novelists and playwrights. Now Spanish domination, hand in hand with reactionary bigotry, spread to the Po valley, and artistic taste resented its encroachments. The writer most representative of this phase is appropriately a Neapolitan, Giovàn Battista Marino (1569-1625). A gifted craftsman, he convinced himself that admiration must be secured at all costs. Through his example preciosity and poetical fireworks, familiar in Spanish and other literatures, became the touchstone of art; and Marino had many imitators. Like most of his contemporaries he scintillates over a vast surface rather than impresses by depth. Of all his writings, lyrics, letters and epic, the *Adone* with its sensuous lilt is the most representative. None of his numerous imitators reached his level. He evinces a wide knowledge of Greek and Latin poetic art, and, like most writers of this age, was learned and highly skilled in technique. These men realized that something was amiss with their own art, and many in Italy, no less than in France, unable to set an example by great works of their own, wrote treatises on the art of poetry. Never was the *Epistola ad Pisones* so frequently imitated.

Through their admiration of the Greeks, Chiabrera, Menzini, Testi, Guidi, and Filicàia were able to offer some resistance to the spread of preciosity. Chiabrera was helped also by his imitation of some metres used by Ronsard and the *Pléiade*, just as Stigliani found a source of inspiration in his personal bitterness against Marinò. But those poets fare better who did not shut their eyes to the political conditions of their country, as, in some of their poems, Chiabrera and Testi. Francesco Redi, again, (1626–98), a learned physician and zoologist, was widely read in old Italian poetry, and though he failed to attain distinction in most of his work, he struck a happy vein in a famous dithyrambic poem, *Bacco in Toscana.*

Literature, no less than manners and men, were in this century steeped in pretentiousness. Alessandro Tassoni (1565–1635), a strong character and a nimble intellect, attacked pretentiousness under all its forms: he pilloried in a heroicomic poem (*La Sècchia rapita*) chevaleresque and epic poems; he criticized Petrarch and his imitators; he even dared to inveigh in eloquent if anonymous orations against the all-powerful Spaniards. Heroicomic poetry enjoyed a great vogue. If the age was not able to rise to the heights of serious art, it knew how to take its revenge and laugh artistically at all that had hitherto been appreciated most highly. Thus, as Tassoni heaped ridicule on heathen gods and knights, Francesco Bracciolini (1566–1645) took mythology as his principal target (*Lo Scherno degli dei*). Tassoni's imitators were many, and many more those whose sole purpose in writing was to raise a laugh. And while the majority laughed, a few nobler spirits satirized in serious verse the errors of the time; chief among them were the painter Salvatòr Rosa (1615–73), large-minded and highly gifted, Menzini, and Sergardi.

Tragedy could not flourish under such conditions; *Adamo*, by the actor Giambattista Andreini, is perhaps the least unworthy of notice. Comedy was restricted to the *commèdia dell' arte*, wherein the usual masks appeared, and actors found scope for their ability in improvisation, skilfully adapting themselves to the tastes of their varying audiences. Pastoral drama thinned into vapid imitation of the older models, and was gradually displaced by musical opera. Society, which during the sixteenth century had enjoyed roaming in search of adventures at Ariosto's bidding, or had been entertained by Bandello's *novelle*, now found those works unpalatable and fed upon tales of little merit but florid in the meretricious glitter of preciosity, or upon novels imitated from the French.

Some of Tassoni's writings show him more keenly attracted by the realities of life than by mere artistic skill, and in truth, while imaginative literature was rapidly declining, the new intellectual life of the Italian nation was inspiring prose works of lasting merit, such as those of Sarpi and Paruta.

The principle of authority, which had been strengthened by the Council of Trent, had already provoked revolt in one great man, Giordano Bruno. Now a Friulian monk, Pàolo Sarpi (1552–1623), trusting to Venetian protection, wrote a history of the Council of Trent in solid, clear, logical prose; and though none can boast of equal merits of style, other historians, like Pàolo Paruta, Cardinal Sforza Pallavicino, Caterino Dàvila, and Daniello Bàrtoli, wrote pages of clear and effective prose.

Circumstances were unfavourable to outspoken political writers; thus, Tassoni was forced to conceal his name when he published his *Filippiche*. But political thought was not extinct, and the example of Venetian freedom and of the unceasing efforts against the foreigners by the Duke Charles Emmanuel I of Savoy raised hopes in the hearts of the best. In Piedmont, at the end of the preceding century, Giovanni Botero had argued that absolute monarchy was the best form of government; now Traiano Boccalini (1556–1613) inveighed against literary and political stagnation and against the absolute rule of the Spaniards. Bernardino Telèsio and Tommaso Campanella also challenged the principle of authority, but the most effective blow came from the works of Galileo Galilei (1564–1642), the champion in Italy of experimental method; his scientific writings are a model of logic and of style, and he revealed his literary pre-dilections in a somewhat bitter criticism of the works of Tasso.

In so far as the century is to be considered a period of literary decadence, it is well represented on the whole by Marino; but it must be borne in mind that literature in these days was not a channel for the real and more active currents of thought. The later Renaissance had been a period of perfection in which all thought had found artistic expression; during the seventeenth century, on the contrary, we find in pure literature only the decline of traditional artistic forms and the echoes of the violent conflict of ideas. The principle of authority was attacked by scientists and philosophers, and even poets took part in this onslaught upon the system that made progress, and the very idea of progress, impossible. During the early part of the eighteenth century the struggle between authority and freedom, between tradition and the experimental method, in fine, between the ancients and the moderns, becomes more intense ; foreign influences are felt more profoundly ; the theories of Descartes and Locke are accepted, discussed, or opposed. And while men were acquiring a clearer notion of the issues at stake, the forces striving for supremacy evinced their diverse peculiarities.

Philosophers maintained that literary works should be true and useful ; academies and periodicals discussed similar questions. In 1690 the academy of Arcadia was founded in Rome. In days when the classics were often better known through modern imitations than in the original, and when Theocritus was the most admired of Greek poets, the academicians of Arcadia endeavoured to heal the disease of decadence by suppressing its symptoms rather than by removing its causes. They set up an artificial pastoral simplicity in opposition to preciosity, and were consequently neither true to nature nor in the direct line of progress. They succeeded, however, in ridding poetry of conceits, but the advance, as appears from the poems of Rolli, Manfredi, or Frugoni, affected the form, not the spirit. It was at this period that Metastàsio (1698–1782) transformed the librettos of musical operas into tragedies observing Aristotelian rules, that Pièr Jàcopo Martelli (1665–1727) wrote tragedies in imitation of the French classics, while Scipione Maffei (1675–1755) returned to the strictest adherence to the unities, and Antònio Conti (1677–1749) attempted to imitate Shakespeare. None of these had yet struck the note of deliverance from rhetorical rule or tradition; though Metastàsio, with the aid of a musical rhythm and by an instinctive insight into the human heart, succeeded in writing moving scenes, though Conti endeavoured to open out new horizons, and though Galiani and Lorenzi composed a charming *libretto* set to music by Paisiello.

Science, vigorous and progressing as it was, was unable to lend a hand to literature. Full of the spirit of the time, captivated by the poetry of knowledge, the new school was indifferent to formal beauty. G. B. Vico (1668–1744), an original philosopher, rose from philological research to a history of human thought (*Scienza nuova*), of great significance, but written in language obscure and difficult; and Lodovico Antònio Muratori (1672–1750) introduced scientific method into historical and literary studies.

While Vico had struck a new line in the philosophy of history, Muratori, indomitably active, helped to establish modern learning upon solid foundations. The former indulged in the most daring speculations, the latter put trust only in original and authentic documents; but neither was a writer of artistic merit. Muratori, who compared favourably with the great contemporary scholars of Flanders and France, promoted literary research by his work and his example. And all this learning, these speculations, this work of research, were seeds that soon bore fruit.

The Rise of the Nation

DURING the sixteenth century Latin had lost its hold as a language, though of course not as a literature. The struggle against the principle of authority in politics, in life, in philosophy, in history and in art, continued with increasing success, under varied forms. The hour of triumph was approaching.

The drama had begun early to shape itself on French models ; so had the novel ; the great philosophers and scholars of the seventeenth century came to Italy from or through France. Everybody who was of any account took pains to learn French ; some even began to look farther afield and grapple with English. The reaction against all that was ancient and traditional, the assertion of a modern mind opposed to ancient, mediaeval, or Renaissance conceptions, cut men adrift from their wonted moorings. For example, Vico created a new philosophy of history in order incidentally to show that modern conceptions of life could be reached from the works of the ancients ; but he remained isolated, and his contemporaries took to studying the literature of other countries. Hence translations began to abound : Conti translated Pope's works, Rolli Milton's *Paradise Lost*, Michele Cesarotti rendered Macpherson's ' Ossian ' and Gray's *Elegies* into Italian verse. But far more important was the influence of French literature. It was the time when in France, in order to avoid the traditional mythology, it was fashionable to invent Persian, Indian, Chinese, and Japanese heroes. It was a fashion that commended itself

to Italians. Letters were written from all sorts of foreign
countries, and in imitation of Montesquieu and Voltaire
the greatest freedom of criticism was indulged in. Savèrio
Bettinelli (1718–1808) treated of the state of learning in
Italy during the Middle Ages and in his *Lèttere virgiliane*
attacked even Dante in his endeavour to cast down all
the literary idols at whose shrines Italians had worshipped
and had acquired, according to him, both the habit of
pedantry and the inability to create a modern literature
of their own. Scientists like Francesco Algarotti
popularized Newton's discoveries; Thomson's *Seasons*
and Young's *Night Thoughts* were translated, French was
spoken and written. Galiani (1728–87) wrote in French
a work on political economy, and a newspaper in French
was printed at Bologna in 1761. Later, German literature
was studied.

Among the leaders of this modernizing movement
were young men like the brothers Pietro and Alessandro
Verri and Cèsare Beccaria, who issued a newspaper at
Milan entitled *Il Caffè* (1764–6) with the avowed purpose
of raising the standard of literature and of acquainting
Italians with current ideas. According to those writers
both ends could be obtained only by breaking free from
tradition, by disregarding all precepts about purity of
language and style, and by studying foreign, especially
French, works. They were true to their own teaching ;
their writings were modelled on the French style and
reeked of Gallicisms; so that their critics were justified
in saying that they had coarsened the Italian language and
defiled it with barbarous words.

Thus, during the second half of the eighteenth century,
two schools of writers could be clearly distinguished, both
exaggerating their defects in the heat of the struggle. for

while the traditionalists, with Savioli, Gherardo de' Rossi, and Jàcopo Vittorelli, did not cease to pipe their mellow pastoral songs, the modernists rejected almost the whole of the literary tradition.

The next stage begins with Giuseppe Parini (1729–99). A peasant-born priest, he started his career with Arcadian poems. Living in Milan as tutor in a noble family, he had before his eyes the idle frivolity of the rich, of which he gives us an ironical description in a highly polished poem, *Il Giorno*; in this poem and in his public-spirited odes he wedded purity of language and style to expression of modern ideas: the man and the poet are one.

In Parini the thought is lofty and intense, its expression is studiously controlled and subdued. In Vittòrio Alfieri (1749–1803) not only is the thought virile but the expression is forcible. A nobleman of Turin, he refused to adapt himself to the frivolous ignorant life of his class; after a wild youth he travelled and studied; comparing the present political weakness of Italy to the glories of the past, he convinced himself that no glory and literature could exist where there was no freedom. He conceived the plan of writing tragedies as a means to spur Italians to action, and at the same time waged war against the oppressors of freedom and the invaders of his country. His attacks were directed also against foreign influence on Italian literature. Now that imitation of foreigners had served its purpose, Alfieri, no less than Parini, saw that there was need not merely of a reform in language and thought but of a loftier temper and profounder thought. He is the apostle of neo-classicism. He observed all the unities, and he drew from his love for the classics fresh inspiration for his attack upon despotism. He was in Paris between 1787 and 1792; he had greeted the

Revolution with joyful anticipation, but when he saw its excesses he ascribed them to the French character and indicted them in his *Misogallo*. His tragedies suffer both as pure literature and as drama from being inspired by political animus; but their meaning may be better valued by reading the poet's autobiography, vivid as a novel, by comparing them with other works staged at that time, and by measuring their undeniable influence upon later writers. Plays, autobiography, satirical poems, lyrics, prose writings are all cast in one mould—a burning ideal of freedom, too exalted to be immediately realized, but such as to fill Alfieri with an artistic scorn no less for those too weak to rebel than for those who turned freedom into violent or cunning abuse.

Alfieri had chosen tragedy not merely as a means of expressing his thoughts, but also because he had observed how weak Italian literature was in this form of the drama. The conditions that had always prevented the rise of tragedy in Italy still prevailed, while comedy was as popular as ever. Carlo Goldoni (1707-93), who had lived among actors, realized that the *commèdie dell' arte* had become outworn and barren. Plays of this type were hardly more than repetitions of traditional motives, and their scope was limited because of the fixed characters of the masks. An artist of kindly disposition, with scarcely any political bias, Goldoni aimed at technical improvement, at putting on the stage character plays, and thus bringing the drama nearer to life and enabling the author to exercise some influence on life and manners. This conception he carried out, even though he was obliged to sacrifice artistic perfection and polish. His output was truly phenomenal. He sometimes imitated Molière, but without sinking his own individuality, and he always endeavoured to delineate characters that were at once true to life and morally elevating.

Modern thought had thus rapidly found its way into the realm of poetry, into both tragic and comic drama ; and after a struggle it prevailed everywhere. The antagonism that Goldoni had to face was perhaps the fiercest. In Venice, where he staged them, his comedies were received very favourably, but playwrights like Chiari did not willingly surrender, and there were many who still preferred the old-fashioned plays, teeming with unforeseeable adventures. They explained Goldoni's success by the novelty of his methods and maintained that any novelty, however insipid, could enforce attention. To prove this contention Carlo Gozzi wrote his charming fairy-tales, the ancestors of *The Blue Bird* and *Peter Pan.* Goldoni's reform did not meet with the approval of the most pugnacious critic of the time, Giuseppe Baretti (1719–89), a man of keen if not unerring judgement, and of great activity and honesty. Versed in several languages and much travelled, Baretti in a periodical, *La Frusta letterària* (1763–5), openly strove to bring about the reform of Italian literature, and so added his weight to that of Parini, Alfieri, and Goldoni. In a series of biting articles he rated the vapid poetry of his contemporaries, contrasting it with the work of foreign writers which deserved to be known in Italy. A friend of the redoubtable Dr. Johnson, he blamed and praised as freely as his English model. He disliked Goldoni and found Dante obscure ; he admired Shakespeare and did not flinch from attacking Voltaire. His prose is rapid and effective, if it is far from having Johnson's balance. In some ways he was the eye of the new era, and he brought to the notice of Italians works little known across the

Alps, and ideas as yet unfamiliar.   Even when his judgement was at fault what he said provoked discussion and served a useful purpose.   Saner than Baretti, more learned, but less inspiring and effective, was Gàsparo Gozzi (1713–86), the author of the periodical *L'Osservatore*, modelled on Addison's *Spectator*.   This Venetian critic dealt with a number of subjects, mainly philosophical or literary, showing himself fully alive to the requirements of the new age, but still unable to renounce stylistic refinement for the sake of effect.   His works include some polished satirical verses in the manner of Parini.   The poetry as well as the prose of this period aimed at some useful purpose ; even Casti, who had deservedly an evil reputation, made a pretence of satirizing the court of Catherine II of Russia and morals in general, and a whole galaxy of poets were laboriously composing didactic poems on scientific subjects.

The sciences were still in the glamour of novelty ; Galileo's discoveries and method had provoked ecclesiastical persecution ; after his death his fame increased, as the principles of freedom for which he had stood gained ground. Though Pietro Giannone (1676–1748) had suffered exile and imprisonment because he had proclaimed the intervention of the Church to be illegitimate in civil matters, others, who called him and Vico their masters— Genovesi, Spedalieri, Filangieri, and Pagano—put forward theories no less daring ; at Milan, Beccaria and Verri subjected criminal law to a searching examination.

Literary criticism and historical method had still to be set on the right lines.   Muratori and Tiraboschi exercised their acumen merely in the ascertaining of facts, others planned historical works of a scope beyond their knowledge and power.   But all this ferment of research, this

activity of original investigators, had succeeded in acquainting the more advanced classes in Italy with the
principles of the makers of the French Revolution.
When revolution came, and overturned government and
constitution, the ideas which it embodied fell in Italy
upon ground well prepared.   During the French Revolution the armies fought, invaded, and pillaged for the sake
of *liberté, égalité*, and *fraternité*.   Thus an idealistic
principle served as a disguise for the permanent desire for
supremacy and gave it powerful aid.   The adversaries of
the French were compelled to have recourse to a similar
alliance : on the one hand, the armies had taken the field,
on the other there had opened the literary warfare in which
the issues were either directly discussed or assumed as
the premisses of the argument ; and victory or defeat in
the field had each its counterpart in the debate which
went on concurrently.

Italians, who have been often undeservedly extolled
for their keen political sense, have never been able to
adapt themselves to the blend of idealistic principles and
practical materialism that was devised at the beginning
of the nineteenth century.   Completely cynical they
could be, or completely idealistic ; but the union of the
two antagonistic tendencies has in general struck them
as incongruous, and their keen logical sense, quick
at detecting any action inconsistent with the pre-
tended idealistic position, has urged them to instant
reaction.

Alfieri, who was a modern, too strong and passionate
to restrain his criticism within the limits of Parini's dis-
dainful smile, inveighed against the French Revolution,
which he had at first greeted with enthusiasm, when he
realized that the deeds of the revolutionaries were not in

strict accordance with their theories. Italians had been stirred to great hopes. The nation, oppressed and divided, had deluded herself into a certainty of freedom and unity—a certainty doubly assured by the fact that Napoleon, the sword of the Revolution, was born in an island geographically Italian, and was of Italian stock. But unity was violated by the sale of Venetia to Austria, and Italy instead of freedom secured only a change of oppressors. The disappointment was the more bitter because of the great hopes to which it succeeded. Ugo Niccolò Fòscolo, born at Zante, but a Venetian by family and by ties of affection (1778–1827), voiced this disappointment. The grief that urges the hero in his novel *Ultime lèttere di Jàcopo Ortis* is not caused by love only, as in Goethe's *Werther*, but also by the calamities of his country; and, as Jàcopo was really a portrait of Fòscolo himself, Italians felt their own anguish to be expressed in this work, soon to become famous. When the French in their democratic fury prohibited tombstones of any kind, endeavouring to force *égalité* upon the dead as upon the living, Fòscolo retorted with one of the finest poems of Italian literature, *I Sepolcri*. He spoke not in the name of tradition, but as the defender of man's most intimate feelings, as a modern who refuses to stifle his own affections or to forgo the life of poetry. Later he tried, with less success, to defend mythology in *Le Gràzie*, and in all his other works, poetical or critical, he expressed in dignified and eloquent language the views of a liberal of the new order. Towering above his fellows by his real critical genius, and helping not a little towards making literature the mouthpiece of sincerity and towards widening men's outlook, Fòscolo, like Alfieri and Parini, was a strong man, a leader of

men, and a pioneer. In contrast with him, Vincenzo
Monti (1754–1828) is typical of the generality of his
contemporary countrymen, unprepared for the outburst
of the Revolution, impressed by its ideals and disgusted
by its excesses, swayed by conflicting emotions and
endeavouring to find their equilibrium amongst the rapid
sequence of events by a compromise of ideals. Endowed
with great literary ability and with an easy and harmonious
turn of verse, he wrote Arcadian lyrics, tragedies,
allegorical, didactic, and historical poems, a translation of
the *Iliad*, and works of criticism. He was easily carried
away by his models, by the fashion of the moment, and
by the desire to please those in power, and he symbolizes
in his work the uncertain state of the Italian mind both in
politics and in letters.

With Alfieri, Parini, Fòscolo, and Monti form had
reverted to classical tradition ; foreign influences had
served their purpose by widening the outlook of literary
men, and by bringing them nearer to life and reality, but
language and style could not be borrowed from òther
countries ; they must be native. The minor poets and
prose writers, such as Ippòlito Pindemonte (1753–1828),
were mainly classical in form, sometimes even in their
matter and their sources. Nor was this change un-
conscious : numbers of books on the Italian language
were appearing, by Monti, Giùlio Perticari, Antònio
Cèsari, and G. F. Galeani Napione ; purity of diction and
freedom of adaptation were advocated in turn ; the claims
of the writers of the fourteenth and of the sixteenth
century to be taken as models for modern writers were
hotly debated, until the time when Manzoni, both by
precept and example, definitely established the language
spoken in Tuscany as the language of literature.

Pietro Giordani (1774–1848), learned, kindly, large-hearted, liberal in politics, modern in spirit, was nevertheless purely classical in taste and style; his influence, far greater than his work, gives him a right to a place among the leading prose writers, and historians like Carlo Botta (1766–1835), Vincenzo Cuoco (1770–1823), and Pietro Colletta (1775–1831), may be classed with him.

All these belonged to the movement of reaction. Napoleon, whatever his actions, had stood as the representative of revolutionary ideas. In 1815 the Congress of Vienna had wound up his affairs and gone back to the principle of authority; the privileged classes, who had formerly acted as a check upon governmental authority, weakened by the Revolution, were unable to offer a resistance; it was therefore only the rising middle classes that succeeded by their enterprise in gradually stemming the reactionary tendencies of governments, and literature faithfully echoes this condition of things, traditional in outward form, full of promise within, yet vitiated by the necessity for compromise. At a time when the great call for reform raised in the late eighteenth century still lingered in the ear, the mere production of literature could not but appear a barren thing, and only writers of mediocre attainments took part in them, while forces began to be marshalled for a fresh literary struggle.

Revolutionary excesses and Napoleon's downfall had brought about the sweeping reaction of the Holy Alliance. But the middle classes were not to be denied, and governments were forced to initiate liberal reforms; the upheaval of revolution subsided into the calm progress of evolution. Revolution had attempted to free men from bondage, whether political, religious, or intellectual. Human energy seemed to have exhausted

itself in this desperate effort, and men were now seeking
refuge once more in religion and in metaphysics, as if
anxious to anchor themselves to principles that were
independent of human passions. They did not, however,
forget the ideas that had recently penetrated their minds,
and sought in religion and philosophy those parts that
were more akin to revolutionary thought. From exalting
man to the pinnacles of divinity, they turned to exalting
the human element in religion. The serene composure
of the classics was antagonistic to their troubled spirits.
Classics and classicism were felt to be heathen, their
religious creations to be outworn and therefore formal
and lifeless. With the reaction against classicism went
the study of mediaeval literature and history, which
seemed wholly permeated by Christianity. These re-
formers called themselves romanticists as against
classicists. It has been said that Christianity has been
always romantic.

The movement did not originate in Italy, but was
brought into the country when it had already triumphed
in Germany and in France. Whatever its sources and
its causes in other countries, it found in Italy a congenial
atmosphere, and it assumed there features of its own. It
became essentially a struggle against the lesser neo-
classicists, who toyed with classical mythology, surrendered
to political reaction, and exhausted their limited powers
in the pursuit of a pure Italian language.

The programme of the Italian romanticists was the
struggle against these tendencies, and therefore it was in
essence the natural continuation of the struggle of which
Baretti, Goldoni, Alfieri, Parini, and Fòscolo had been the
heroes, producing a literature that dealt with things and
ideas rather than words, a language modern and effective

rather than conformed to the standard of fourteenth-century models, and an aspiration towards political freedom, unity, and independence.

Experience and maturity had brought moderation into political ideals. The programme that we have just outlined was not, however, clearly defined in the minds of its promoters. Great struggles and violent clashes of ideas had occurred in neighbouring countries. The Italian romanticists believed themselves to be far more revolutionary than they actually were. And the discussion as to their aims that raged principally at Milan, the very same town in which *Il Caffè* had been published half a century earlier, was so many-sided as to be confused, and in the end it was found that the romanticists had hardly any opponents apart from reactionary governments, because the whole literary world had become imbued with modern ideas and spoke a modern language. The result was that the movement gradually became essentially political.

The organ of the romanticists, *Il Conciliatore*, was published at Milan (1818–19). Among its contributors were Giovanni Berchet, who had started the debate upon the romantic movement in 1816 by his *Lèttera semisèria di Grisòstomo*, the jurists G. D. Romagnosi (1761–1835) and Melchiorre Giòia (1767–1829), and Sìlvio Pèllico (1789–1854), whose *Francesca da Rìmini* (1815) had met with great success rather because of its transparent liberal tendencies than on account of any literary merit.

The most gifted recruit of the new school was Alessandro Manzoni (1785–1873), a scion of a rich and noble family, a strong character, of moderate views, and well balanced. He had been praised by Fòscolo and Monti for his early works. During a long stay in Paris

(1808–10) he had passed through a deep, great, moral and literary crisis. In Paris he wrote a poem, *In morte di Carlo Imbonati*, in which truth and virtue are set forward as the objects of literary art. He had once inclined to religious scepticism, but he became an ardent Catholic and, as if to proclaim his conversion, he composed his religious *Inni* (1816–22), highly lyrical poems, in which he endeavoured to bring back to religion human feelings that naturally arise from it. At the death of Napoleon I he composed an ode, *Cinque Màggio*, which Goethe praised and translated, and about the same time he wrote two historical tragedies, *Il Conte di Carmagnola* and *Adelchi*, which survive mainly on account of their inspired lyrical sections and of their outspoken liberalism.

In a letter to a friend in 1826 Manzoni laid down the principles of his art, which were accepted with applause by all who called themselves romanticists in Italy—*l'ùtile per iscopo, il vero per soggetto, l'interessante per mezzo.*

Meanwhile it had become apparent to all that the romantic compromise between the principle of authority and revolutionary thought was merely a transient phase. Other European countries were battling for freedom and some were on the point of securing it; in Italy the advanced patriots (*Carbonari* and *Giòvane Itàlia*) were active, and revolutionary risings took place. These were rapidly suppressed by Austria or her retainers; the savagery of reaction was unleashed and revealed what the essence of romanticism was. Berchet had to flee to London; Pèllico was seized and suffered eight years' imprisonment in an Austrian dungeon, an experience which he related in his book *Le Mie prigioni* (1832). From now onwards the struggle for Independence becomes fiercer, and reactionary measures are blindly merciless. According to the territorial states in which they lived and wrote, and according to their personal character, Italian writers are more or less outspoken, insinuating or denunciatory, satirical or despairing, but the whole of the literature throbs with the expectation of events that are imminent : oppression is doomed.

In 1827 Manzoni brought out his historical novel *I Promessi sposi*, in which the patient suffering of the lower classes under Spanish rule during the seventeenth century is depicted with supreme art, and in which contemporary readers were quick to detect allusions to events more recent. Historical novels were written by Tommaso Grossi ; with greater artistic effect and a stronger political appeal by Màssimo d'Azèglio (1798–1866) ; in a rhetorical style but more outspoken, as was possible under the more tolerant government of Tuscany, by Francesco Domènico Guerrazzi (1804–73). Tragedies having an evident political purpose were written by Giovàn Battista Niccolini (1782–1861) ; and lyrical poems were sung in countless numbers.

It is remarkable that the greatest poet of the time, Giàcomo Leopardi (1798–1837), seems to stand apart from the general movement. By native tendency, as well as by the rule under which he was born, and by family circumstances, his judgement upon moral and metaphysical matters was perverted. Yearning for affection, he was deprived of family affection and of love ; centring his whole life upon study and learning, he was by ill health denied any but the most limited and painful occupation ; steeped in the doctrines of French philosophers, he lived in a bigoted household and under the rule of the pope ; craving for beauty, he was made by infirmity almost

repellent to look at ; athirst for intellectual companion-
ship, he pined in isolation in an uncultured town, or if at
the cost of much suffering he undertook long journeys
failed to find the object of his search ; ever naturally
conscious of his own gifts and abilities, he moved among
his contemporaries receiving from them but scant apprecia-
tion. The romantic movement seemed to him barren,
because it added little to and failed to improve upon the
achievements of the great writers of the late eighteenth
century ; the new spirit of hope in politics which imbued
his contemporaries appeared to him infantile, living as he
did under the more stringent rule of the papal government
and inclined by nature to exaggerate the lessons to be
drawn from the failures of the several liberal movements
he had witnessed. His mind soared far above immediate
events. Whether in verse or in prose he echoed the grief
of humanity confronted by unsurmountable difficulties ;
the optimistic tendency of the age angered one who
could see no glimmer of hope ; and thus he became
the most bitter critic of the compromise upheld by
romanticists, and he rose above the immediate problems
and vicissitudes of his day to the contemplation of man's
fate, holding himself for the most part aloof from political
matters. Therefore his *Operette morali*, like his marvellous
Canzoniere, are a lamentation over human suffering and
decadence, as well as the echo of a grief filling one who
was keenly alive to the sorrows and to the errors, but
not to the yearnings and the strivings of his countrymen.

A poet much inferior to Leopardi, but in close touch
with his contemporaries, Giuseppe Giusti, a Tuscan by birth
(1809–50), viewed with scorn the false position into which
fictitious concessions had led the so-called constitutional
governments during the thirties and forties. The Tuscan

was perhaps, with the exception of the Piedmontese, the least oppressive of Italian governments, and its attempts at reform lent themselves to ridicule. Giusti was a patriotic writer, fully in sympathy with his age; the difference of his style and tone from those of most of his contemporaries cannot be ascribed to the causes that acted on Leopardi, but rather to his personal leanings to satire, and to the influence of other poets of the time who were no less inclined to burlesque than he was. Among them are Filippo Pananti, who shrank from politics and lived many years in London, Antònio Guadagnoli, and Arnaldo Fusinato.

Between 1821 and 1848 liberalism gradually ceased to be a merely intellectual movement, and became a programme of action; riots, plots, and insurrections, untimely but recklessly daring, kept political passion at seething point; the Austrian government and its Italian retainers, compelled by this threatening attitude of the more cultured classes who rapidly gained favour with the people, resorted to measures of violent repression. The list of Italian martyrs increased, and their sufferings helped to stir hatred and patriotic feeling among the least combative citizens. A succession of poets—political exiles or soldiers of liberty—endowed the plotters and insurgents with battle songs or passionate outbursts against the enemy. Gabriele Rossetti (1783-1854), the inspirer of the Neapolitans during the insurrection of 1820, was compelled to seek refuge in England. Berchet in his *Fantasie*, and the Modenese Pietro Giannone (1792-1872) in his *Èsule*, recounted the secret labours of the *carbonaro* and the torments of exile; Alessandro Poèrio, a serious poet, was killed during the siege of Venice, and Goffredo Mameli, a youth whose lyrical poems are sung with enthusiasm to this day, died of wounds at Rome in 1848. .

Other writers wedded patriotic feeling to lachrymose romanticism ; such were Giovanni Prati (1814–84), at times forcible though often only facile and sonorous, Antonio Gazzoletti, and Tommaso Grossi.

The strengthening of national sentiment also brought dialectal literature to the front ; Grossi himself wrote political satires in Milanese, but he was surpassed by his fellow-citizen Carlo Porta (1776–1821), who with a superficial meekness portrayed in his poems the suffering of the people during the successive dominations of France and Austria, while Gioachino Belli (1791–1863) drew a faithful and facetious picture of life in Rome, before 1849, as well among the poor as among the clergy and aristocracy.

All these, on a higher or lower level, were calling Italians to action ; and especially the young, women, and old people were experiencing in the sadness of their homes the counter-effects of political activity and persecution, and were driven to find solace in romantic poems and harrowing tales ; Grossi, Prati, Càrcano, and Cantù provided such grains of comfort, as well as d'Azèglio and Guerrazzi, whom we have already mentioned.

In a history-making epoch, fond of historical novels, history was naturally in great favour. Later there appeared autobiographical sketches by d'Azèglio, by the sculptor Giovanni Duprè, and the pseudo-autobiographical novel by Ippòlito Nievo (1831-61), the *Memòrie di un ottuagenàrio*, in which life in Venetia before and after the downfall is vividly described. In Florence there appeared the *Stòria del reame di Nàpoli* by Pietro Colletta, *Stòria del Vespro siciliano* by Michele

Amari, both southern political exiles, and the *Sommàrio della stòria d'Itàlia* by Cèsare Balbo (1789–1853).

Political writings appeared without number, often of outstanding merit; Giuseppe Mazzini (1805–72), who devoted the whole of his life,—most of it spent in exile,—to the realization of his political ideals, maintained a wide correspondence, by means of which he directed the action of the secret society *Giòvane Itàlia*. But his unceasing activity was by no means restricted to letter-writing; he was in a sense the embodiment of romantic politics; the compromise between religion and revolution was set forth by him in his motto *Dio e pòpolo*; and he put faith rather in insurrection than in any other means to secure freedom and unity for his country. His innumerable writings are all fraught with a burning passion for the Italian people and for all enslaved nationalities. He proved himself to be a seer, so truly have later events justified some of his views; and, because he was gifted with extraordinary insight, his critical and literary essays, written in a clear, crisp style, are worthy to rank with the best.

A republican like Mazzini, Carlo Cattàneo (1801–69) did much, by his political and his literary activities, to bring about the revolution at Milan in 1848; while Giuseppe Ferrari echoed Vico's philosophy of history and Pasquale Galluppi and Antònio Rosmini gave themselves to metaphysical speculation. The most important of all these scholars, only second to Mazzini perhaps in political effectiveness, was Vincenzo Gioberti (1801–52), who, during his exile in Brussels (1843), being equally devoted to Italy and to the Roman Church, imagined the possibility of an Italian confederation under the pope, and, conceiving a perfect nation and a perfect Church, wrote

Del primato morale e civile degli Italiani—a work which, both because it flattered and encouraged Italians, only too accustomed to being castigated by their impatient leaders, and because it sketched a hopeful and apparently attainable programme, was hailed with tempestuous enthusiasm and became the Italians' Bible for the years preceding 1849.   When the events of that year proved that the Church at least was not capable of assuming the functions that Gioberti had assigned to it, nothing daunted, he composed *Il Rinnovamento civile degli Italiani*, urging Piedmont to take the lead in uniting Italy, and he was preparing a philosophical treatise against the Church, when he was interrupted by death.

Gioberti brings us to the wars that made Italy.   In these days of rapid development, the leadership was taken by Camillo Benso di Cavour, who was already known as an acute political writer.   For the time literature seemed to be awaiting events.

Modern Italy

From 1815 to 1848 Italians set their national problem before their own eyes and before the eyes of Europe. These were years of preparation. The romanticists recalled the glories of past ages and described the miseries of serfdom ; Gioberti proclaimed the right of Italy to be independent and drafted a new constitution ; Mazzini untiringly called for action.   The risings of 1848 and 1849 showed, by their failure, that the means by which the solution of the problem had been attempted were inadequate.   But they also pointed the way to other means, for the forces had been marshalled, and the end had been shown to be attainable. The helm passed to other hands; Piedmont, led by Cavour with unerring skill, from a provincial state became the heart of Italy, the kernel of the future kingdom. It offered itself for martyrdom in the cause of national unity; it took part in the Crimean War; it paid for France's intervention in 1859 by the cession of two of its provinces, Nice and Savoy. Italy's cause had justice on its side, and in spite of Austrian opposition, in spite of insufficient preparation and threatened European complications, it triumphed. In 1859 Napoleon III had arrested the victorious armies of France and Piedmont before Venetia could be freed, but, though Prussia succeeded in this manœuvre, she could not prevent central Italy in 1860 from joining the new state, nor Garibaldi from completing his historic expedition from Sicily to Naples. Political dissensions weakened the state, but the war between Prussia and Austria in 1866 allowed Venetia to be liberated, though incompletely, despite the fact that inefficient leadership caused both the gallant army and the gallant navy to be defeated. Again, the war between France and Prussia in 1870 brought the opportunity to suppress the temporal power of the pope, to occupy Rome, and to bring Italy to practical if not complete unity.

When compared with the actual results, the toll paid in securing these goals seemed but light; political skill and good fortune were credited with the success, rather than military valour or real strength. Perverse politicians made much of this contention, and in the face of the heavy financial burdens the national spirit was depressed. Austria by possessing the Trentino and Julian Venetia still

held the gates of invasion ; allies had shown themselves not to be trusted ; conflicting interests and adherence to past political ideals caused France to be
unfriendly to the new kingdom ; an alliance with the old
enemy, Austria, became unavoidable, an alliance which
moved many of the best Italians to utter disgust and
fostered a cynical scepticism ; later on, unfortunate checks
to colonial expansion in Abyssinia confirmed the worn-
out generation that had succeeded the makers of Italy
in their distrust of the powers and the destinies of the
state.

The long-sustained wave of enthusiasm that had made
possible sacrifice, martyrdom, secret agitation, rebellion,
and victory, of a sudden subsided. The dream of
centuries had become reality, but the reality had none
of the rosy splendour of the dawn. A rapid swing
towards realism, a decadence of romanticism and of
religion, a return to traditional classicism—all this followed as a matter of course.

The impetus of the earlier movement, however, could
not be abruptly stopped ; especially in a country having
no one intellectual centre, or rather having several
centres, each of which in turn claimed, and still claims,
pre-eminence.

Thus plaintive romanticism had still its devotees :
among them Prati (1814–84), its most celebrated exponent,
and Aleardo Aleardi (1812–96), mellow, ' sensible ', but
lacking strength of every kind. Niccolò Tommaseo (1802–
74), a Dalmatian, who had come to Italy, plotted, fought,
and suffered exile and imprisonment for the cause of
liberty, infused into romanticism a mystic strain, much of
his learning, and some of his native ruggedness. Emilio
Praga (1839–75), a Bohemian dreamer, wedded imitation of

French to ideas of his own; Arrigo Bòito (1842–1918), a famous composer, hammered his rhymes with infinite care and consummate mastery and attempted to carry his readers into a world of phantastic gloom; while Francesco dall' Òngaro (1810–73) aimed, with an affected simplicity, at a sort of romantic Arcadia. Each was adding some new element to a literary movement which was hastening to inevitable decadence—a decadence, however, by no means complete or final, as is shown by the works of Fogazzaro, Butti, and others.

Giosuè Carducci (1835–1907) sounded the clarion of the anti-romantic revolt; yet he owed much to Victor Hugo and Heine. A whole-hearted patriot, he inveighed with violence against the dishonesty of politicians, and seems to speak with the voice of the Italian conscience during the years 1860–90. His scorn of the romanticists was unlimited and outspoken. They were responsible, in his opinion, for seducing the Italian mind to resignation and compromise, to a detachment from realities which rendered corruption possible, and for introducing into literature a sentimentality foreign to the native character, and vagueness of form not to be reconciled with the definite contour of a sunlit landscape.

This reaction against romanticism Carducci informed with his own personality, and, because with him there started a tendency of which the ultimate consequences are still apparent, it seems necessary to observe it more closely.

Learned in the classics, forceful and rugged, country-born and a worshipper of nature, he identified his goddess with the rich and fertile soil of the Italian plains or with the wind-swept hills of Tuscany, and he loathed the mistiness of romanticism, which he identified with religion, and religion he identified with the clergy and the papacy. His crusade, therefore, was against all that hindered the enjoyment of nature as gloriously embodied in Italy—a crusade which he fought in many volumes of essays and verses.

His is not the classicism of Alfieri or Fòscolo or Parini; though his philosophical creed can hardly be said to differ from that of the French Encyclopaedists. Living in an age beset with political problems, and deeply interested in the events of history, it was inevitable that he should allow his muse to dwell on such subjects as were familiar to him, but the substance of his doctrine must be sought in his *Inno a Sàtana*, in which reason is exalted as self-sufficient, and in his *Canto dell' amore*. His historical poems, though numerous, are merely incidental; his political invectives are violent because they are not cramped by pessimism; but the real meaning of his works and of his teaching is the revival of a vigorous Latinity, antithetical to misty vagueness, pervaded with sunlight and with the joy of life in perfect communion with a benign nature.

Most of his early contemporaries were carried away by his robustness, like Giovanni Marradi, the more dreamy Severino Ferrari, or the homely Guido Mazzoni; or were overshadowed by him, like the neo-classic Giàcomo Zanella (1820–88) and the realistically sensuous Olindo Guerrini; or, if they were opponents, like the philosophical Màrio Rapisardi, they were dwarfed by his personality. His clarion call raised many other echoes. Translations were no longer confined to foreign masterpieces; the barriers of tyranny and oppression, which had kept in isolation the majority of Italians, if not their leading spirits, were swept away, so that alongside the main national movement there could be traced others having their sources across the Alps or beyond the sea. If these may be left to explain themselves, another movement, which came to a head towards the end of the century, claims fuller treatment. Francesco de Sanctis (1818-83), a scholar well read in philosophy and in literature, who had been exiled from Naples by the Bourbons, became the most famous of Italian critics and the founder of a school of criticism; his essays and his *Stòria della letteratura italiana* struck a new line; his keen insight and his philosophical mind rendered him the more readily interested in probing the motives of literary works than the details of their authorship and composition. While Carducci reacted against uncertainty of vision in creative literature, de Sanctis endeavoured to establish criticism on a philosophical basis and revolted against the looseness of criticism that is merely personal and instinctive. His method demanded a learning and gifts that are granted to few; but his works helped his contemporaries to understand the main currents of literature and perhaps to grasp the meaning of Carducci's aims, at least in its negative aspects. Drama developed independently; popular taste favoured the historical or problem plays of Pàolo Ferrari (1822-89), the romantic dramas of Pàolo Giacometti, ·Leopoldo Marenco, Giuseppe Giacosa (1847-1906), or the historical tragedies of Pietro Cossa (1830-81). Novelists were late in striking an individual note.

In the last decades of the nineteenth century the kingdom of Italy was still endeavouring to find its way. It was the same causes of dissatisfaction that were diverting the course of political events from the natural tendencies of the people, and that evoked in literature either cynical realism, or the effort towards a more intimate communion with nature. Foreign literatures, French, German, and Russian, were making their influence felt upon individual writers.

Lyrical poetry, however, developed on national lines. Carducci's peculiar classicism affected Gabriele d'Annùnzio in his early youth. His first collections of poems as well as his later *Làudi* express the fullness of joy, complete absorption in nature; the poet revels in an Arcadian orgy and labours untiringly in the lavish adorning of the white-hot expression of his emotions: some parts of his poems are unsurpassed for sincerity of thought and artistic finish.

Giovanni Pàscoli (1855–1912), senior in years to d'Annùnzio, matured less rapidly and represents a later development of the same movement. Lacking the energy of the younger man and his power of sensuous enjoyment, he was readier to listen to mysterious voices of nature. It seemed as if poetry, sated by sounds, light, colours, and passions, was seeking for shady spots and quiet scenes. For Pàscoli nature is no longer the provider of sensuous joy, but the consoler in a world beset by man-made troubles and pervaded by mysteries of the other world. He does not endeavour to embrace nature as a whole, but rejoices in drawing from the peaceful contemplation of it all the contentment it can give to a sensitive mind. Professedly a rationalist, he may in some of his moods be likened to Wordsworth, and in some to Poe.

Carducci had often introduced historical personages in his patriotic songs; Pàscoli likewise could not be deaf to the popular passions during the colonial wars, but he was hardly fitted to enter into the fray of battle, for his spirit was above human hatred. In contrast with them, d'Annùnzio, during the war in Libya and the Great War, was fired with the primitive lust for blood. The beautiful country in which he was born, on the glory of which he had feasted his eyes, could be habited only by a conquering people. Thus even his war songs, crowded with historical allusions, are the outcome of the poetical movement which reached in him its highest mark. Progress in Italy as in other countries brought into prominence the social conditions of the working classes, and Ada Negri (b. 1870) was moved to revolt by the dreariness of their lot. Antònio Fogazzaro (1842–1911), sincerely religious, could not shut his ears to the voices of the beyond, and followed in the path of the romantic tradition. Arturo Graf (1848–1913) expressed his inborn pessimism with subtle refinement. Local characteristics or popular customs inspired gifted dialectal poets, such as the Tuscan Renato Fucini, the Roman Cèsare Pascarella, the Neapolitan Salvatore di Giàcomo.

Poets may claim to interpret popular aspirations, sometimes to anticipate them, but with few exceptions their influence, in Italy at least, is restricted to a small circle of readers. A wider appeal may be claimed by novel-writers and playwrights; and, as they are more eager than poets to meet the popular taste, their testimony may be considered more significant. Manzoni's novel had arisen from a rare combination of gifts; writers who attempted to follow in his steps either fell into old-fashioned romanticism or spiritless description of commonplace existence; perhaps Emìlio de Marchi (1851–1910) alone may be said to have had some success in this line. Lighter in tone, and concerned rather with providing amusement than lasting works, were, among others, Antòn

Giùlio Barrili and Salvatore Farina, both of whom endeavoured to keep aloof from political or religious strife. A follower of Manzoni, equally optimistic but lacking in depth, Edmondo de Amicis (1846–1908), the favourite of the young, laboriously minute, seemed to infuse into his descriptive writing something of the pliability of his own mind, more ready to compromise than to fight.

The teaching of Zola, who had attempted to write scientific novels on the experimental system, found a certain following among Italian writers, who were also at the same time unconsciously influenced by the lyricism of the time. Each discovered for himself a setting, a province in which nature and men were most familiar to him, and therefore more easy to describe. To this were due Giovanni Verga's powerful Sicilian tales, Gràzia Deledda's gloomy and monotonous pictures of Sardinia, Matilde Serao's stories, fluent but without vigour, mostly about Neapolitan life. Geròlamo Rovetta (1851–1910), because he lived among the busy middle classes, found in them his subjects, and his cynical tragedies of money-grasping financial magnates are documents of contemporary life ; Marco Praga, the son of Emìlio, told the same story almost as effectively.

Among novel-writers d'Annùnzio stands alone. A poet rather than a novelist, he gives admirable local descriptions, he writes pages of glittering prose, but his characters, unless they are the true children of instinct, or unless they portray the complicated experiences of a lust-ridden hero, lack the breath of real life, and seem only to express the varying intellectual attitudes of d'Annùnzio himself. A man of wide reading, and very sensitive to intellectual and artistic influences, he was in turn captivated by the French decadents, the Russian pessimists, the philosophy of Nietzsche; and the fanciful heroes engendered by such influences talk rather than live; they are swayed by the will to conquer and the thirst for pleasure, but are never capable of suffering. He generally chose to set the scene among fashionable society, and thus deprived himself of a really national background. Yet his novels are throbbing with energy, and in them we see the beginnings of a new development; his heroes, who were in his earliest novels merely epicurean and intro-spective, in the later books become active. The author, temperamental as he is, gave the first sign of a new epoch, even before men were aware of its approach.

The same may be said of the other novelist who shared with d'Annùnzio the principal place during the last decades of the nineteenth century. Fogazzaro, who of course has nothing but fame in common with d'Annùnzio, by nature inclined to vague meditation, a lover of music and of a religious temperament, appeared in his youth as a legitimate descendant of the romanticists, with a leaning towards some of their recent German followers; tearful scenes, lily-white death-ridden young ladies are the heroines of his early novels; the happy course of love is thwarted by death in affecting circumstances. The heroes of his stories, if above the normal human stature, are for the most part extraordinarily impressive. In the later stages of the development of his art, Fogazzaro succeeded in expressing through his men and women the conflict between materialistic science and reawakening religious thought, with pictures boldly sketched from the life and shrewd observations upon human character.

The classical reaction had exalted nature and science over against religion and the spiritual life; political disappointment had thriven in a cynical atmosphere where any compromise in act, creed, or opinion was not felt to jar. At last Italian minds were growing restive; they were no longer sceptically indifferent to any but practical problems; they were wandering once more in search of a philosophy that should encourage and satisfy. Fogazzaro indicated his solution in the harmony between science and religion, and made this the subject of his more famous novels; and he wove his threads amidst historical surroundings, thus linking himself with the romanticists of the early years of the century. The rush of spiritual life was so irresistible, that not only Fogazzaro felt it, but even d'Annùnzio became sensitive to it (*La Contemplazione della morte, La Leda senza cigno*, &c.), and Pàscoli, as has been said already, walked for many years on the confines of mystery listening to voices that he could not by mere reason understand.

A similar change could be seen in the drama. Romantic plays or pleasant entertainments gave way for a time to adaptations or imitations from Sardou; then Rovetta, Praga, Sabatino Lopez, Giannino Antona-Traversi, and Roberto Bracco described or satirized the cynical despondency of the period, not independently of the pessimism of Ibsen, Hauptmann, Sudermann, and Strindberg; later, new life and greater energy appeared in plays by Rovetta (*Romanticismo*), by Giuseppe Giacosa (*Come le fòglie*), and by others. At the same time dialect drama passed beyond the simple staging of local scenes and customs, to a deeper significance in the plays of the Venetian Giacinto Gallina (1852–91).

D'Annùnzio himself held the stage, winning admiration by his magical literary skill. His best plays are, however, his earliest (*Gioconda, La Fìglia di Iòrio*): in his later attempts to portray great historical moments, he succeeded rather in staging dazzling pageantry than in breathing real life into his characters.

Side by side with creative literature developed criticism. Between 1860 and 1890 there flourished a number of notable men of letters, politicians, and amateur philosophers, more akin to Sainte-Beuve and Taine than to Vico; among them were Ruggero Bonghi, Alessandro Chiappelli, and Gaetano Negri. Alfredo Oriani (1852–1909), a more original and profound thinker than these, produced some striking political writings full of learning and instinct with the national spirit, such as *Fino a Dògali* and *La Lotta polìtica in Itàlia.*

Before the wars of independence, history, political and literary, had been studied but superficially; even de Sanctis' example disposed lesser critics rather to rapid conclusions than to patient research, though in Germany Adolf Gaspary and others were prompted by him to more serious studies. In Germany, in fact, the great movement for scientific research was by now in full force, and gifted German scholars had applied the historical method also to subjects connected with mediaeval and Renaissance Italy. The method was not new, for it had been pursued by Lorenzo Valla in the fifteenth century, and Muratori in the eighteenth (with a large following, Tiraboschi, Quadri, &c.). Carducci, Alessandro d'Ancona, Adolfo Bàrtoli, Graf, Francesco d'Ovìdio, and Pasquale Villari practised it and preached it. A group of patient and highly gifted researchers set to work; in a remarkably brief period of time manuscripts and documents were edited; learned periodicals were founded in quick succession (among them the *Archìvio stòrico italiano,* the *Giornale stòrico della letteratura italiana,* and the

Bullettino della società dantesca are the most compre-
hensive). No less than in Germany the whole field of
research was covered by a system of reviews and learned
societies. But the Germans had made a dubious present
with their scientific methods. In Germany itself there
soon appeared a machine-made pedantry and the worship of historical method as an end in itself; and in Italy
its barrenness, when not coupled with special abilities,
soon became apparent. While political depression and
spiritual dearth lasted, it became a refuge for painstaking
scholars, but as soon as the revival in creative art began
to show itself, a great réaction set in. Just as art could
not be merely realistic description, criticism could not be
mere worship of documents. The historical method had
rendered great service; but learning and scholarship
needed to be brought into relation with social activity.
Hitherto they had been restricted to a relatively small
section of professional students; now social conditions
and political aspirations made it necessary that scholars
should infuse life into their teaching and make it more
spirited and more acceptable to the multitudes that
thirsted for knowledge.

Benedetto Croce (born 1866) was the leader of this
purely idealistic movement; profoundly versed in historical method, he linked his works to those of de Sanctis
and Vico. He expounded, moreover, a complete philosophy; his *Estètica* exerted a very great influence upon
men of letters. The age was ripe for the reform. No
sooner was it announced than the best among professional
scholars were influenced by it, while a number of young
men championed it with a vigorous onslaught on earlier
methods. Some of them naturally went too far in their
belittling of scholarship, and many of their writings are

mere pleadings for indolent and captious criticism, but the struggle was necessary in order to stamp out pedantry and to render criticism alive to its obligations to the community. Through Croce, Giovanni Gentile, and their followers, interest in philosophy was revived, so that during the last years of the nineteenth century works on philosophical and religious themes were published, and at the present time there are many students working and writing on such subjects.

At last Italians were recovering from their political disappointment. Long years of thrift and industry had brought better economic conditions; with a consciousness of strength there arose a feeling of hope, and with hope a keener sensitiveness to pain and grief. Italians had patiently borne many a bitter humiliation from friends and foes; they were no longer in the mood for bearing more. Alfredo Panzini, the most resigned of modern writers, was showing in his novels and short stories the real strength and the weaknesses of the middle classes; he brought out their sufferings and their strong qualities of hopefulness, activity, and poetic vision. D'Annùnzio was ready to give the signal for action; Enrico Corradini, Giùlio de' Frenzi, and their friends excited national pride; Croce had linked scholarship to its Italian sources and fostered a sense of confidence and strength; Oriani, called to new fame by Croce, revealed to Italians the inner history of their political development; Vilfredo Pareto expounded the reasons of social progress.

For half a century new Italy had feared lest she were really old; she had felt oppressed by the long ages of conflict and agony; now at last Italians, like the Italians of Mazzini and Gioberti, felt young in strength though they knew themselves to be the descendants of the famous Italians of the past. The increase of wealth, commercial and industrial activity, and the progress of agriculture enhanced this sense of youthfulness.

The new Italy now looked forth upon the world, conscious of her own fresh beauty and newly acquired strength, proud of her lineage and of her past, but impatient of admirers who, enraptured by her ancient glory, were indifferent or blind to her present possibilities.

Another movement arose, inspired by the extreme worshippers of the present. They called themselves futurists; they claimed to be independent of all earlier schools, and yet they were echoing some of d'Annùnzio's Nietzschian strains, as much as they were profiting by attacks levelled against pedantry by the followers of Croce. They had a negative programme; the suppression of the past, of the memory and study of dead artists and writers; monuments, masterpieces, and museums were their pet aversions; their positive programme was the expression of the energy that they felt and realized in the people of the age. Wealth, and the wealth-building machinery of industry, motion, as the expression of energy, noise, dust, war, were held up to unique praise. Laws, morals, religious systems were scoffed at as useless restrictions upon the free development of the new era and having their foundations in past ages. The rebellion was the more violent because it attacked some of the most cherished and popular ideals, and, being violent and excessive, it succeeded more in its negative than in its positive programme. Gradually some of the most gifted of the sympathizers of the movement stood aside from it, and enriched literature with works of great promise and profound significance.

Free from tradition, or at least not shackled by.

excessive subservience to tradition, these writers, most of them in touch with the daily press, were able to unfurl the banner of new ideals and to keep it flying. There appeared a thinker like Prezzolini, a writer subtle, learned, effective like Giovanni Papini. The latter, a pragmatist in philosophy, by his series of vivid essays, sometimes paradoxical but always thoughtful and candid, became a leader of public opinion. His prose, lucid, fresh, and limpid, even though sometimes falling into a perverse affectation of vulgarity, exemplifies along with that of Panzini, Morselli, and Sòffici the best modern style.

Thus, while a host of playwrights, essayists, and novelists, too numerous to mention, were amusing, educating, and speaking for the new generation, while criticism, well informed and perspicacious, was interpreting art and literature in a spirit liberated from slavish adherence to foreign methods, while philosophers were debating the claims of pure idealism, or of pragmatism, against positivism or other older systems, while a number of reviews and of daily papers were making for further progress, the Great War broke out. But progress was not checked; with meritorious courage publishers and editors carried on. Many a young writer of promise fell fighting. No one who is not conversant with their works can appreciate the loftiness of self-sacrifice and of human ideals with which the real leaders of the Italian mind, the young men, went to the war. From their works alone can we conjecture whether the glory of the deeds accomplished, or the disillusionment caused by the return to a world of political jealousies, or the pride of having given all for the sake of justice, is to inspire the literature of the near future.

List of Authors and their Works

THIS list is appended for the guidance of readers who may wish to read any of the principal works of authors named in the text. It is arranged in the order in which the names of the authors occur for the first time in the text, the works of each being collected together, though often cited in different passages.

The numbers printed in Clarendon type refer to the page or pages on which works are mentioned or discussed. A few works are also given of authors who may be classed with those mentioned in the text, though they are not directly cited. Titles of Latin works are placed in square brackets. Neither the list of authors nor that of the works of each author aims at completeness. The editions cited have been selected with a view to their accessibility to English readers. When the name of an editor is added it means that notes are provided, but SL, SC, CC, BES, BSS, CE, BE, TE are all plain texts.

For each period a few anthologies are given in which specimens of the works of different writers are to be found.

Readers desiring information as to critical works on particular authors or points of biography or bibliography should consult the monumental work *Stòria letterària d'Itàlia scritta da una società di professori*, Milan, Vallardi, 1900–18, the *Manuale della letteratura italiana* by Professors A. d'Ancona and O. Bacci, Florence 1903-11, or smaller works such as *Stòria della letteratura italiana ad uso dei licei* by Professor Vittòrio Rossi, Milan 1910, *Compèndio di stòria della letteratura italiana ad uso delle scuole secondàrie* by Professor Francesco Flamini, Leghorn 1919, or *Le orìgini e lo svolgimento della letteratura italiana* by Professor Michele Scherillo, Milan 1919 (only vol. i published). *La stòria della letteratura italiana* by Francesco de Sanctis, Bari 1913, should be read by all who wish to gain an insight into the spirit of Italian literature.

LIST OF ABBREVIATIONS

SL. Scrittori d' Itàlia, published by Gius. Laterza e figli, Bari.
FL. Clàssici della filosofia moderna, publ. by Gius. Laterza e figli, Bari.
SC. Scrittori nostri, publ. by R. Carabba, Lanciano.
CC. Cultura dell' ànima, publ. by R. Carabba, Lanciano.
BES. Biblioteca clàssica econòmica, publ. by E. Sonzogno, Milan.
BSS. Biblioteca scolàstica di clàssici italiani, publ. by G. C. Sansoni, Florence.

CE. Clàssici italiani, publ. by Istituto editoriale italiano, Milan.
BE. Breviari intellettuali, publ. by Istituto editoriale italiano, Milan.
TE. Biblioteca del teatro italiano, publ. by Istituto editor. ital., Milan.
CV. Clàssici italiani annotati, publ. by F. Vallardi, Milan.
CH. Biblioteca clàssica hoepliana, publ. by U. Hoepli, Milan.
BR. Bibliotheca romanica, publ. by J. H. Ed. Heitz (Heitz & Muendel), Strasburg.
IN. Collezione di clàssici italiani con note, published by Casa editrice Lapi, Città di Castello, and the Unione tipogràfico-editrice torinese.

I. THE DAWN
A. ANTHOLOGIES.

Crestomazia italiana dei primi sècoli per Ernesto Monaci, Città di Castello, 1889–1912.
Manuale della letteratura del primo sècolo di Vincenzo Nannucci, Florence 1878.
L. Piccioni, *Da Prudènzio a Dante, Manuale di stòria della lett. ital. dei sècoli IV–XIII*, Turin 1916.
The Forerunners of Dante, a selection from Italian Poetry before 1300 edited by A. J. Butler, Oxford 1910.
Rimatori sìculo-toscani del dugento. A. Zaccagnini, A. Parducci. SL. 72.
Antica lìrica italiana (canzonette, canzoni, sonetti dei sècoli XIII e XIV). G. Carducci, Florence 1907.
Rime di Cino da Pistòia e di altri del sècolo XIV. G. Carducci, Florence 1862.
Letteratura italiana. Stòria ed esempi. T. Casini, Rome-Milan 1907.
Fiore di leggende. Cantari antichi. E. Levi. SL.
Leggende del sècolo XIV. I. del Lungo, Florence 1863.
Rime di trecentisti minori. G. Volpi, Florence 1907.
Cantilene e ballate, strambotti e madrigali dei sècoli XIV e XV. G. Carducci, Pisa 1871.
Cacce in rima dei sècoli XIV e XV. G. Carducci, Bologna 1896.
Poemetti mitològici dei sècoli XIV e XV. F. Torraca, Leghorn 1888.
Lamenti stòrici. A. Medìn, L. Frati, Bologna 1887—Padua 1894.

B. SINGLE AUTHORS.

Le cento novelle antiche (Il Novellino). E. Sicaidi, BR.; also A. Marenduzzo. CV. 10.
Jacopone da Todi, *Le Làude.* G. Ferri. SL. 8.
Guido Cavalcanti, *Rime.* E. Checchi. SC. 9.
Lapo Gianni e Gianni Alfani, *Rime.* E. Lamma. SC. 10.
Dante Alighieri, *Tutte le òpere.* E. Moore, Oxford 1904. 10, 13.

Dante Alighieri, *La Vita nuova.* G. Melodia, CV; M. Scherillo, CH.
   La Vita nuova e il Convìvio (Excerpta). F. Flamini, Leghorn
   1910.
   La Commèdia. F. Torraca, Rome–Milan 1908; also G. A.
   Scartazzini, G. Vandelli, Milan 1914.
   [De vulgari eloquentia. De monarchia. Epistolae. Eclogae.]
Cecco Angiolieri, *I Sonetti.* A. F. Massera, Bologna 1906. II.
I Fioretti di San Francesco. A. della Torre, Turin 1909. II.
Francesco da Barberino, *Del reggimento e costume die donna.*
   Bàudi di Vesme, Bologna 1875. *I Documenti d' amore.*
   F. Egidi, Rome 1902 (unfinished). II.
Bartolomeo da S. Concòrdio, *Gli Ammaestramenti degli antichi.*
   V. Nannucci, Florence 1846. II.
Guido da Pisa, *I Fatti di Enea.* A. Marenduzzo. CV.
Dino Compagni, *La Crònica.* I. del Lungo, Florence 1902.
   La Crònica, le Rime e l'Intelligenza. R. Pìccoli. SC. II.
Giovanni e Matteo Villani, *Le Crònache,* Triest 1858. II.
Cino da Pistòia, *Rime.* D. Fiodo. SC. 10–11.
Jàcopo Passavanti, *Lo Spècchio di vera penitenza.* G. Polidori,
   Florence 1856. II.
Caterina da Siena, *Lèttere.* N. Tommaseo, Florence 1860.
   Libro della divina dottrina. M. Fiorilli. SL. II.
Francesco Petrarca, *Il Canzoniere.* G. Rigutini, M. Scherillo. CH.
   1908.
   Il Canzoniere e i Trionfi. A. Moschetti. CV. 1908.
[Africa. De viris illustribus. Rerum memorandarum libri. De
   contemptu mundi. De ocio religiosorum. De vita solitaria.
   De remediis utriusque fortunae. Itinerarium syriacum. De
   sui ipsius et multorum ignorantia. Eclogae. Epistolae (Ital.
   trans. by G. Fracassetti : *Familiari,* Florence 1859; *Senili,*
   Florence 1869). II–14.
Giovanni Boccàccio, *Il Decamerone.* M. Scherillo. CH 1914;
   also CE.
   Òpere minori. I. Moutier, Florence 1827–34.
   Antologia delle òpere minori volgari. N. Zingarelli, Naples
   1913.
   Il Filòstrato. P. Savj-Lopez. BR.
   Ninfale fiesolano. B. Wiese, Heidelberg 1913.
   Amorosa visione. D. Ciàmpoli. SC.
   La Fiammetta. G. Gigli. BR.
   Il Corbàccio. L. Sorrento. BR.
   [De genealogiis. De casibus. De claris mulieribus. De
   montibus. Bucolicon carmen.]
Fàzio degli Uberti, *Il Dittamondo,* Milan 1826.
   Lìriche èdite ed inèdite. R. Renièr, Florence 1883. 14.
Federico Frezzi, *Il Quadrirègio.* E. Filippini. SL. 14.
Ser Giovanni Fiorentino, *Il Pecorone* (15 tales). G. Papini.
   SC. 15.

Giovanni Sercambi, *Novelle*, Bologna 1871. 15.
Franco Sacchetti, *Il Trecentonovelle*, London 1795, also Milan 1804 and BES. 15.
Pieràccio Tebaldi, *Le Rime.* S. Morpurgo, Florence 1885. 15.

II. THE RENAISSANCE

A. ANTHOLOGIES.

Letteratura italiana. Stòria ed esempi. T. Casini, Rome-Milan 1909.
Manuale della letteratura italiana. A. d'Ancona, O. Bacci, Florence 1903–10.
Prosa e prosatori. Della prosa volgare del quattrocento. O. Bacci, Palermo 1907.
Lìrica italiana antica. E. Levi, Florence 1905.
Lìrica italiana nel cinquecento e nel seicento. E. Levi, Florence 1909.
Cantilene e ballate, strambotti e madrigali dei sècoli XIV e XV. G. Carducci, Pisa 1871.
Cacce in rima dei sècoli XIV e XV. G. Carducci, Bologna 1896.
Lamenti stòrici. A. Medìn, L. Frati, Bologna 1887—Padua 1894.
Poemetti mitològici de' sècoli XIV e XV. F. Torraca, Leghorn 1888.
Sacre rappresentazioni dei sècoli XIV, XV e XVI. A. d'Ancona, Florence 1872.
Poeti umanisti maggiori. L. Grilli. IN.
Raccolta de' satìrici italiani. G. Càrcano. Turin 1853.
Lìrici del sècolo XVI. BES.
Commèdie del cinquecento. I. Sanesi. SL.
Trattati d'amore del cinquecento. G. Zonta. SL.
Trattati del cinquecento sulla donna. G. Zonta. SL.
Novellieri minori del cinquecento. G. Gigli, F. Nicolini. SL.
Riformatori italiani del cinquecento. G. Paladino. SL.
Economisti del cinque e seicento. A. Graziani. SL.
Luigi Pulci, A. F. Doni, G. Simeoni, F. Berni, F. Bracciolini, J. Cicognini, F. Baldovini, Clàsio, G. Gozzi. *Poemetti contadineschi.* SC.

B. SINGLE AUTHORS.

Colùccio Salutati [*Epistolario*]. F. Novati, Rome 1891-6.
Pòggio Bracciolini [Poggii epistolae]. T. Tonelli, Florence1 832. 19.
Leonardo Bruni [Leonardi Bruni Arretini epistolarum libri octo]. L. Mehus, Florence 1741. 19.
Ambrògio Traversari [Ambrosii Traversari epistolae]. P. Canneto, Florence 1759. 19.
Francesco Filelfo [*Cent-dix lettres grecques*]. E. Legrand, Paris 1892. 19.

Gasparino Barzizza [Gasparini Barzizii Bergomatis et Guiniforti filii opera]. G. A. Furietti, Rome 1723. **19.**
Lorenzo Valla [De voluptate. Dialecticae disputationes. Historiarum Ferdinandi Regis libri tres. Elegantiarum latinae linguae libri vi]. **19.**
Flàvio Biondo [Blondi Flavii Historiarum ab inclinatione Romanorum libri xxxi]. Bâle 1559. **19.**
Marsilio Ficino [Marsili Facini opera]. Bâle 1576. **20.**
Giovanni Pontano [I. I. Pontani Carmini]. B. Soldati, Florence 1902. **19.**
Angelo Poliziano, *Òpere volgari.* T. Casini, Florence 1885.
 Prose volgari inèdite, poesie latine èdite ed inèdite. I. del Lungo, Florence 1867.
 L' Orfeo e le Stanze. F. Neri. BR.
 Le Stanze, l' Orfeo e le Rime. CE. **20.**
Leonardo Giustiniàn, *Poesie èdite e inèdite.* B. Wiese, Bologna 1883. **20.**
Lorenzo de' Mèdici, *Poesie volgari.* J. Ross, E. Hutton, London 1912.
 Poemi. G. Papini. SC.
 Canti carnascialeschi. CE. **20.**
Serafino Aquilano (S. De' Ciminelli dall' Àquila), *Le Rime.* M. Menghini, Bologna 1894 (incomplete). **21.**
Cariteo (Benedetto Gareth), *Le Rime.* E. Pèrcopo, Naples 1892. **21.**
Matteo Maria Boiardo, *Orlando innamorato.* F. Fòffano. Bologna 1906-7, and also CE.
 Poesie volgari e latine. A. Solerti, Bologna 1894. **21, 22.**
Galeazzo di Tàrsia, *Il Canzoniere.* F. Bartelli, Cosenza 1888. **21.**
Luigi Tansillo, *Poesie èdite ed inèdite.* D. Fiorentino, Naples 1882.
 L' Ègloga e i poemetti. F. Flamini, Naples 1893. **21.**
Vittòria Colonna, *Rime e lèttere,* Florence 1869. **21.**
Verònica Gàmbara, *Rime e lèttere.* P. Mèstica Chiappetti, Florence 1879. **21.**
Gàspara Stampa e Verònica Franco, *Rime.* A. Salza. SL. **21.**
Verònica Franco, *Terze rime e sonetti.* G. Beccari. SC. **21.**
Luigi Pulci, *Il Morgante.* G. Volpi, Florence 1900-4. **22.**
Lodovico Ariosto, *Orlando Furioso.* P. Papini, Florence 1903; also expurgated, P. Micheli, Milan 1908; also CE.
 Le Sàtire. G. Tàmbara, Leghorn 1903; also C. Berardi, Campobasso 1918.
 Commèdie e sàtire. CE.
 Elegie, sonetti e canzoni. A. Sòffici. SC. **23, 26, 28.**
Teòfilo Folengo (Limerno Pitocco, Merlìn Cocai), *Òpere italiane.* U. Renda. SL.
 Le Maccheroneę. A. Luzio. SL. **23.**

Giàn Giòrgio Trìssino, *L'Itàlia liberata dai Goti*, Venèzia 1729.
  La Sofonisba tragèdia e i Simìllimi commèdia, Milan 1864.
  24, 27.
Luigi Alamanni, *Versi e prose.* P. Raffaelli, Florence 1859. 24.
Bernardo Tasso, *Amadigi*, Venice 1560. 24.
Torquato Tasso, *Gerusalemme liberata.* S. Ferrari, Florence 1890;
  also CE. 24.
  Òpere minori in versi. A. Solerti, Bologna 1891-5.
  Rime. A. Solerti, Bologna 1898-1902.
  I Discorsi dell' arte poètica, il Padre di famìglia, l' Aminta.
  A. Solerti, Turin 1902.
  L' Aminta e il Torrismondo. CE. 24, 27, 28.
Gentile Sermini, *Novelle.* A. Colini. SC. 26.
Sabbadino degli Arienti, *Le Porrettane.* G. Gambarìn. SL. 26.
G. B. Giraldi, *Gli Ecatommiti*, Turin 1853. 26, 27.
Sebastiano Erizzo, *Le Giornate*, Turin 1853. 26.
Matteo Bandello, *Novelle.* G. Brognòligo. SL. 26.
Niccolò Machiavelli, *Il Prìncipe.* G. Lìsio, Florence 1900; also
  L. A. Burd, Oxford 1891.
  Il Prìncipe e le Deche. CE.
  Istòrie Fiorentine, Florence 1872.
  Lèttere. SC.
  L' Arte della guerra. BE.
  Scritti minori. BE.
  La Mandràgola. S. Debenedetti. BR. 26, 29.
Àgnolo Firenzuola, *Prose scelte.* S. Ferrari. BSS. 26.
Antòn Francesco Doni, *I Marmi.* P. Fanfani, Florence 1863. 26
Luigi da Porto, *Giulietta e Romeo.* CE. 26.
Antòn Francesco Grazzini (Il Lasca), *Le Cene.* C. Verzone, Florence
  1890.
  La Sibilla. G. Papini. SC.
  La Strega. G. Papini. SC. 26.
Bernardo Dovizi da Bibbiena, *La Calàndria*, Milan 1863. 26.
Lorenzino de' Mèdici, *L' Aridòsia e l' Apologia.* F. Ravello, Turin
  1916; also CE. 27.
Francesco d' Ambra, *Commèdie*, Triest 1858. 27.
Giovàn Maria Cecchi, *Commèdie inèdite.* G. Tòrtoli, Florence 1855.
  Drammi spirituali inèditi. G. B. Rocchi, Florence 1895-1900.
  27.
Annibal Caro, *Òpere*, Florence 1864.
  Prose scelte. M. Sterzi, Leghorn 1909.
  L' Apologia. LE. 27.
Pietro Aretino, *Commèdie.* E. Camerini, Milan 1876.
  *Pasquinate di P. A. o anònime per il conclave e l' elezione di
  Adriano VI.* V. Rossi, Palermo-Turin 1891.
  Un pronòstico Satìrico (MDXXXIV). A. Lùzio, Bèrgamo
  1900.
  Cartèggio (bks. i–ii). F. Nicolini. SL. Also LE, SC. 27, 28.

Giordano Bruno, *Il Candelàio.* V. Spampanato, Bari 1909. Also BR. **27.**

Sperone Speroni, *Òpere,* Venice 1740. **27.**

Jàcopo Sannazzaro, *Arcàdia.* M. Scherillo, Turin 1888. **27.**

G. B. Guarini, *Il Pastòr fido.* C. Orlando. BR, also LE. **28.**

Geròlamo Savonarola, *Sèrmoni e trattati.* BE.
  Poesie, SC. **25.**

Francesco Berni, *Rime, poesie latine e lèttere èdite e inèdite.* A. Virgili, Florence 1885.
  Rime. LE. **28.**

Leòn Battista Alberti, *Il Trattato della pittura e cinque ordini architettònici.* SC.
  Libro della famìglia. G. Mancini, Florence 1908; also LE. **28.**

Giovanni Domìnici, *Règola del governo di cùra familiare.* D. Salvi, Florence 1860. **28.**

Baldesàr Castiglione, *Il Cortegiano.* V. Ciàn, Florence 1910; also LE. **29.**

Giovanni della Casa, *Òpere.* G. B. Casotti, Florence 1907.
  Prose scelte e annotate. S. Ferrari, Florence 1900. **29.**

Giòrgio Vasari, *Vite dei più eccellenti pittori, scultori ed architetti,* Florence, Salani s. a.
  Vite scelte. G. Urbini, Turin 1898. **29.**

Benvenuto Cellini, *Vita.* O. Bacci, Florence 1901; also LE. **29.**

Françesco Guicciardini, *Istòria d'Itàlia,* Turin 1874.
  Òpere inèdite. G. Canestrini, Florence 1857–67.
  Òpere inè lite (Considerazioni sopra ai discorsi del Machiavelli. Ricordi polìtici. Discorsi polìtici), 2nd ed. Florence 1857.
  Ricordi polìtici e civili. G. Papini. CC. **30.**

III. THE TRANSITION

A. ANTHOLOGIES.

Manuale della letteratura italiana. A. d'Ancona, O. Bacci, Florence 1903–10.

Luigi Pulci, A. F. Doni, G. Simeoni, F. Berni, F. Bracciolini, J. Cicognini, F. Baldovini, Clàsio, G. Gozzi. *Poemetti contadineschi.* SC.

Raccolta de' satìrici italiani. G. Càrcano. Turin 1853.

Lìrici marinisti. B. Croce. SL.

Poeti eròtici del sècolo XVIII. G. Carducci, Florence 1868.

Poeti minori del settecento. A. Donati. SL.

Antologia della poesia italiana. O. Targioni-Tozzetti, Leghorn 1899.

Antologia della prosa italiana. O. Targioni-Tozzetti, Leghorn 1898.

B. SINGLE AUTHORS.

Leonardo da Vinci, *Frammenti letterari e filosòfici.* E. Solmi, Florence 1899; also CE. **30.**

Michelàngelo Buonarroti, *Poesie*. G. Amèndola. SC.
  Lèttere. G. Papini. SC.
  Rime e lèttere. CE. **22, 30.**
G. B. Marino, *Adone*, Florence 1886.
  Poesie vàrie. B. Croce, SL.
  Epistolàrio. A. Borzelli, F. Nicolini. SL; also LE. **33.**
Gabriello Chiabrera, *Poesie lìriche, sermoni e poemetti*. G. Polidori, Florence 1865.
  Autobiografìa, diàloghi, lèttere scelte. G. Agnino. SC. **34.**
Benedetto Menzini, *Òpere*, Florence 1731-2.
  Sàtire, London 1788.
Fùlvio Testi, *Òpere scelte*, Mòdena 1817. **34.**
Alessandro Guidi, *Poesie*, Naples 1780. **34.**
Vincenzo da Filicàia, *Poesie e lèttere*. U. A. Amico, Florence 1864. **34.**
Francesco Redi, *Poesie e prose scelte*. A. Pippi, Florence 1895.
  Rime e prose. CE.
  Bacco in Toscana. LE. **34.**
Alessandro Tassoni, *La Sècchia rapita, l' Ocèano e le Rime*. T. Casini, Florence 1887.
  La Sècchia rapita. P. Papini, Florence 1912 ; also CE.
  Rime. T. Casini, Bologna 1880.
  Considerazioni sopra il Canzoniere del Petrarca, Venice 1609.
  Lèttere. G. Rossi, Bologna 1901-10. **34, 35, 36.**
Francesco Bracciolini, *Lo Scherno degli dei*, Milan 1804. **34.**
Lorenzo Lippi, *Il Mamantile riconquistato*, Florence 1861. **34.**
Salvatòr Rosa, *Sàtire*. CE. **35.**
G. B. Andreini, *Adamo*. E. Allòdoli. SC. **35.**
Ruzzante, *La Fiorina*. TE. **35.**
Pàolo Sarpi, *Stòria del Concìlio di Trento*, Florence 1858.
  Scritti filosòfici inèditi. G. Papini. CC. **35.**
Sforza Pallavicino, *Òpere èdite e inèdite*, Rome 1844-8. **36.**
Caterino Dàvila, *Istòria delle guerre civili di Fiandra*, Venice 1733. **36.**
Pàolo Paruta, *Stòria veneziana* (excerpta). G. Paladino. SC. **36.**
Giovanni Botero, *Ragiòn di stato*, Venice 1589. **36.**
Traiano Boccalini, *Ragguagli di Parnaso e Pietra del paragone polìtico*. G. Rua. SL.
  Ragguagli di Parnaso (excerpta). G. Gàbriel. SC. **36.**
Tommaso Campanella, *Poesie*. G. Papini. SC.
  La Città del sole. Aforismi. D. Ciàmpoli. SC. **36.**
Galileo Galilei, *Òpere*, Florence 1890-1901 (*Scritti letterari*, vol. ix).
  Prose. CE.
  La prosa. I. del Lungo, A. Fàvaro. BSS.
  Òpere letteràrie. R. Bàlsamo Crivilli. BES. **36.**
Paolo Rolli, *De' poètici componimenti*, Nice 1782.
  Il Paradiso perduto, Venice 1818. **37, 39.**

Eustàchio Manfredi, *Rime scelte.*   F. Fòffano, Règgio Emìlia, 1888.
37.
Carlo Innocenzo Frugoni, *Òpere poètiche*, Parma 1779.   37.
Pietro Metastàsio, *Drammi scelti.*   CE ; also LE.   37.
Pièr Iàcopo Martelli, *Tragèdie*, Venice 1708.
Fèmia, Bologna 1869.
Scipione Maffei, *Mèrope*, Venice 1747.   37.
Antònio Conti, *Prose e poesie*, Venice 1739.
Le Quattro tragèdie, Florence 1751.
L'Uomo del Pope, Venice 1788.   37, 39.
G. B. Lorenzi, B. Galiani, *Sòcrate immaginàrio, commèdia per
mùsica.* M. Scherillo, Milan 1886.   38.
G. B. Vico, *La Scienza nuova.*   F. Nicolini, Bari 1913 ; also LE.
Le Orazioni inaugurali [De antiquissima Italorum sapientia]
e le Polèmiche. G. Gentile, F. Nicolini, SL.
L' Autobiografia, il Cartèggio e le Poesie vàrie. B. Croce. SL.
Autobiografia e Lèttere. BE.   38.
Lodovico Antònio Muratori, *Epistolàrio.* M. Càmpori, Mòdena
1901-10.   38.

IV. THE RISE OF THE NATION

A. ANTHOLOGIES.
Manuale della letteratura italiana. A. d'Ancona, O. Bacci,
Florence 1903-10.
Poeti minori del settecento. A. Donati. SL.
Antologia della poesia italiana. O. Targioni-Tozzetti, Leghorn
1899.
Antologia della prosa italiana. O. Targioni-Tozzetti, Leghorn
1898.
I Poeti italiani del sècolo xix. R. Barbiera, Milan 1913.

B. SINGLE AUTHORS.
Savèrio Bettinelli. *Prose èdite e inèdite.* G. Mazzoni, Bologna
1882.
Lèttere virgiliane. P. Tommasini-Mattiucci, Città di Castello
1913.   40.
Melchiorre Cesarotti, *Poesie di Ossian antico poeta cèltico*, Florence
1808-11.   39.
Francesco Algarotti, *Òpere scelte*, Milan 1842.   40.
Ferdinando Galiani, *Dialogues sur le commerce des blés*, Paris
1770.
Della moneta. F. Nicolini. SL.
Antologia di tutti gli scritti. F. Nicolini, Bari 1909.   40.
Jàcopo Vittorelli, *Poesie.* A. Simioni. SL.   41.
Giuseppe Parini, *Poesie.* G. Natali, CV ; also M. Scherillo, CH
and CE.
Prose. E. Bellorini. SL.

Guiseppa Parini, *Il diàlogo della nobiltà*. BE. 41-2.
Vittòrio Alfieri, *Òpere*, Turin 1903.
    Scelta di tragèdie e di poesie minori. N. Vaccaluzzo, Leghorn
    1909.
    Prose e poesie scelte. G. Mèstica, Milan 1898.
    Il Misogallo le Sàtire e gli Epigrammi èditi e inèditi. R. Re-
    nièr, Flórence 1884.
    Tragèdie scelte. CE.
    La Congiura de' Pazzi. TE.
    Le Sàtire. BE.
    La Vita. E. Bertana, Naples 1910; also CE.
    Della tirànnide. BE. 41, 42.
Carlo Goldoni, *Commèdie scelte.* CE.
    Le Avventure della villeggiatura. TE.
    Il Ritorno dalla villeggiatura. TE.
    Gli Amori di Zelinda e Lindoro. TE.
    Le Gelosie di Lindoro. TE.
    Memòrie. G. Mazzoni, Florence 1907. Also CE.
    Poesie. BE. 42.
Pietro Chiari, *La Veneziana di spìrito*, Venice 1872. 43.
Carlo Gozzi, *Le Fiabe.* E. Masi, Bològna 1889; also CE.
    La Marfisa bizzarra. C. Ortiz. SL.
    Memòrie inùtili. G. Prezzolini. SL. 43.
Giuseppe Baretti, *La Frusta letterària.* CE.
    Prefazioni e polèmiche. L. Piccioni. SL.
    Discours sur Shakespear et sur Monsieur de Voltaire. F. Bion-
    dolillo. SC.
    La scelta delle lèttere familiari. L. Piccioni. SL 26. 43-4.
Gàsparo Gozzi, *L'Osservatore*, Florence 1889.
    Scritti scelti. CE.
    Lèttere familiari. BE. 44.
G. B. Casti, *Il Poema tàrtaro*, Pisa 1821.
    Gli Animali parlanti, Paris 1802. 44.
Pietro Giannone, *Stòria civile del regno di Nàpoli*, Milan 1823.
    Il Triregno, Rome 1895.
    Vita, scritta da lui medèsimo. F. Nicolini, Naples 1905. 44.
Cèsare Beccaria, *Dei delitti e delle pene*, Florence 1854. 44.
Pietro Verri, *Discorso sulla felicità.* BE. 44.
Ugo Fòscolo, *Òpere èdite e pòstume*, Florence 1850-62.
    Poesie. CE.
    Prose. CE.
    Lìriche scelte, i Sepolcri e le Gràzie. S. Ferrari, Florence 1891.
    Últime lèttere di Jàcopo Ortis. A. Martinetti, C. Antona-
    Traversi, Saluzzo 1887.
    Discorsi Sulla lìngua italiana. BE.
    Lezioni d' eloquenza. BE.
    Prose militari. BE. 46.
Vincenzo Monti, *Lìriche e poemi.* CE.

Vincenzo Monti, *Poesie scelte.* A. Bertoldi, Florence 1891.
  Càio Gracco. B. Cotronei, Messina 1897.
  Lezioni d' eloquenza. BE.
  Epistolàrio. BE. 47.
Ippòlito Pindemonte, *Poesie originali.* A. Torri, Florence 1858.
  47.
Pietro Giordani, *Prose scelte.* G. Chiarini, Florence 1890 ; also CE.
  48.
Carlo Botta, *Stòria delle guerre dell' indipendenza d'Amèrica,*
  Florence 1856. 48.
Pietro Colletta, *Stòria del reame di Nàpoli.* Manfroni, Milan 1905 ;
  also CE. 48.
Vincenzo Cuoco, *Sàggio stòrico sulla rivoluzione di Nàpoli.* F.
  Nicolini. SL.
  Platone in Itàlia. F. Nicolini. SL. 48.
Giovanni Berchet, *Poesie.* E. Bellorini, SL ; also LE.
  Scritti crìtici e letterari. E. Bellorini. SL.
  Lèttera semisèria di Grisòstomo. A. Galletti, SC ; also BE. 50.
Giàn Domènico Romagnosi, *Òpere,* Padua 1841-5.
  La mente sana. BE. 50.
Sìlvio Pèllico, *Prose e tragèdie scelte.* F. d'Ovìdio, Milan 1898.
  Le Mie prigioni e altri scritti scelti. E. Bellorini, Milan 1907.
  Le Mie prigioni. CE. 50, 51.
Alessandro Manzoni, *I Promessi sposi.* M. Scherillo, CH ; also
  LE.
  Le tragèdie, gli inni e le odi. M. Scherillo. CH.
  Poesie. LE.
  Scritti minori. LE. 50-2.
Tommaso Grossi, *Marco Visconti,* Florence 1885. 52.
Màssimo d'Azèglio, *Èttore Fieramosca,* Florence 1885.
  Niccolò de' Lapi, Paris 1842.
  I Miei ricordi. CE. 52.
Francesco Domènico Guerrazzi, *L'Assèdio di Firenze,* Paris 1847.
  Racconti e scritti minori. CE.
  Stòria d' un moscone. BE.
  Autodifesa. BE. 52.
G. B. Niccolini, *Òpere èdite e inèdite.* C. Gargiolli, Milan 1863-80.
  Arnaldo da Brèscia. CE. 52.
Giàcomo Leopardi, *Òpere,* Florence 1845-6.
  Epistolàrio, Florence 1892 ; also BE.
  Scritti letterari, Florence 1899.
  Pensieri di vària filosofia e di bella letteratura, Florence
  1898-1900.
  Scritti vari inèditi dalle carte napoletane, Florence 1906.
  Canti. G. Mèstica, Florence 1886 ; also M. Scherillo. CH
  and CE.
  Operette morali. G. Gentile, Bologna 1918.
  Prose. CE, also BES. 52-3.

Giuseppe Giusti, *Poesie scelte.*   E. Guastalla, Leghorn 1910;
also CE.
Epistolàrio èdito ed inèdito.   F. Martini, Florence 1904.
Lèttere d'amore.   BE.   53–4.
Filippo Pananti, *Opere in versi e in prosa,* Florence 1824.
Il Poeta da teatro, Venice 1843.   54.
Antònio Guadagnoli, *Gli scherzi poètici,* Naples 1831.   54.
Arnaldo Fusinato, *Poesie,* Milan 1868.   54.
Gabriele Rossetti, *Poesie.*   G. Carducci, Florence 1861.
Canti della pàtria.   BE.   54.
Alessandro Poèrio, *Poesie.*   M. d'Ayala, Florence 1852; also
Naples 1860.   54.
Goffredo Mameli, *Scritti èditi e inèditi.*   A. G. Barrili, Genoa
1902.
Lìriche.   CE.   54.
Giovanni Prati, *Poesie scelte.*   F. Martini, Florence 1892.
Canti politici.   BE.   55.
Carlo Porta, *Poesie èdite ed inèdite.*   R. Barbiera, Florence 1894.
Poesie scelte.   BE.   55.
Giuseppe Gioachino Belli, *Duecento sonetti in dialetto romanesco.*
L. Morandi, Città di Castello 1896.   55.
Pietro Buratti, *Poesie veneziane scelte e illustrate.*   R. Barbiera,
Florence 1886.   55.
Giovanni Duprè, *Pensieri sull' arte e ricordi autobiogràfici,* Florence
1880.   55.
Ippòlito Nievo, *Le Confessioni di un ottuagenàrio.*   CE.   55.
Michele Amari, *Stòria del Vespro siciliano,* Milan 1886.   55–6.
Cèsare Balbo, *Sommàrio della stòria d'Itàlia.*   F. Nicolini.   SL.   56.
Giuseppe Mazzini, *Scritti* (ediz. nazionale), Imola 1906.
Scritti scelti.   J. White Mario, Florence 1901.
Scritti letterari.   CE.
Ai giòvani d'Itàlia.   BE.
Doveri dell' uomo.   BE.   56.
Carlo Cattàneo, *Scritti polìtici e epistolàrio,* Florence 1892–4.
Saggi.   BE.   56.
Antònio Rosmini, *Breve schizzo dei sistemi.   Diàlogo su la vera
natura del conòscere.*   C. Caviglione.   CC.
Il Sistema filosòfico.   BE.   56.
Vincenzo Gioberti, *Del primato civile degli Italiani,* Brussels 1843.
Del rinnovamento civile d'Itàlia.   F. Nicolini, SL; also
CE.   56–7.
Camillo Benso di Cavour, *Itàlia, Aùstria e Frància.*   BE.   57.

V. MODERN ITALY

A. ANTHOLOGIES.
D'Ancona e Bacci, *Manuale della letteratura italiana,* 1903–10.
I Poeti italiani del sècolo XIX.   R. Barbiera, Milan 1913.

Antologia della critica e dell' erudizione coordinata allo studio della storia letteraria italiana. F. Flamini, Naples 1915.
T. Grossi, Sestini e Tommaseo, *Novelle in versi.* CE.

B. SINGLE AUTHORS.

Aleardo Aleardi, *Canti,* Florence 1899.
  Poesie. BE. 59.
Niccolò Tommaseo, *Le Confessioni.* BE.
  Roma e il mondo. BE.
  Prose. CE. 59.
Emìlio Praga, *Tavolozza,* Turin 1882.
  Penombre, Milan 1864. 59.
Arrigo Bòito, *Il Libro dei versi—Re Orso,* Turin 1877.
  Nerone, Milan 1907. 60.
Francesco dall' Òngaro, *Stornelli.* BE.
  Il Pòvero Fornaretto. TE. 60.
Giosuè Carducci, *Òpere* (20 vols.), Bologna 1890-1905 (also a popular
    edition with notes).
  Prose, Bologna 1907.
  Poesie, Bologna 1907. 60-1.
Enrico Annìbale Butti, *Il Castello del sogno,* Milan 1910. 60.
Giovanni Marradi, *Poesie,* Florence 1905. 61.
Severino Ferrari, *Versi.* L. Màuri, Turin 1906.
  Il Mago, Turin 1906. 61.
Guido Mazzoni, *Poesie,* Bologna s. a. (1913). 61.
Giacomo Zanella, *Poesie,* Florence 1910. 61.
Olindo Guerrini (Lorenzo Stecchetti), *Poesie,* Bologna 1903. 61.
Màrio Rapisardi, *Òpere poètiche,* Palermo 1912. 61.
Francesco de Sanctis, *Stòria della letteratura italiana,* Bari 1913.
  Sàggio sul Petrarca, Naples 1907.
  Saggi critici, Naples 1866. 62.
Pàolo Ferrari, *Òpere drammàtiche,* Milan 1877-84.
  Teatro scelto, Milan 1890. 62.
Pàolo Giacometti, *Teatro,* Milan 1877. 62.
Giuseppe Giacosa, *Una Partita a scacchi,* Turin 1871.
  Il Conte Rosso, Turin 1876.
  Tristi amori, Milan 1893.
  Come le fòglie, Milan 1900.
  Il Più forte, Milan 1905. 62, 67.
Pietro Cossa, *Teatro in versi,* Turin 1877-83. 62.
Emìlio de' Marchi, *L' Età preziosa,* Milan 1886. 64.
  Demètrio Pianelli, Milan 1890.
Antòn Giùlio Barrili, *L' Olmo e l' èdera,* Milan 1877. 65.
  Come un sogno, Milan 1876.
Salvatore Farina, *Il Tesoro di Donnina,* Milan 1872.
  Mio fìglio, Milan 1879-82.
Gabriele d'Annùnzio, *Primo vere.* SC.
  Intermezzo di rime, Milan 1894.

Gabriele d'Annùnzio, *Làudi*, Milan 1903-12.
   Le Novelle della Pescara, Milan 1902.
   Il Piacere, Milan-1889.
   L'Innocente, Milan 1891.
   Le Vèrgini delle rocce, Milan 1896.
   La Contemplazione della morte, Milan 1912.
   La Città morta, Milan 1898.
   La Gioconda, Milan 1899.
   La Fìglia di Iòrio, Milan 1901.
   Prose scelte, Milan 1906. 63.
Giovanni Pàscoli, *Myricae*, Bologna 1896.
   Poemetti, Bologna 1907.
   Poesie. L. Pietriboni, Bologna 1918.   63.
Ada Negri, *Fatalità*, Milan 1890.
   Tempeste, Milan 1896.
   Il Libro di Mara, Milan 1919. 64.
Antònio Fogazzaro, *Malombra*, Milan 1881.
   Fedele ed altri racconti, Milan 1883.
   Daniele Cortis, Milan 1885.
   Pìccolo mondo antico, Milan 1896. 64.
Arturo Graf, *Medusa*, Turin 1890.
   Le Danàidi, Turin 1905.
   Poemetti drammàtici, Milan 1905. 64.
Renato Fucini, *Le Vèglie dei neri*, Florence 1883.
   Nàpoli a òcchio nudo, Florence 1919. 64.
Cèsare Pascarella, *Sonetti*, Rome s. a. (1904). 64.
Salvatore di Giàcomo, *Teatro*, Lanciano 1910.
   Poesie, Naples 1907.
   Novelle napoletane, Milan 1914. 64.
Edmondo de Amicis, *Ricordi di Londra*, Milan 1873.
   La Vita militare, Milan 1880.
   Alle porte d'Itàlia, Milan 1884. .
   Cuore, Milan 1886.
   La Carrozza di tutti, Milan 1899. 65.
Giovanni Verga, *I Malavòglia*, Milan 1881.
   Novelle rusticane, Turin 1883. 65.
Grazia Deledda, *Racconti sardi*, Sàssari 1894.
   L'Èdera, Rome 1918.
   Il Vècchio della montagna, Milan 1912. 65.
Matilde Serao, *Paese di Cuccagna*, Naples 1910.
   Dopo il perdono, Rome 1918. 65.
Geròlamo Rovetta, *Le Làgrime del pròssimo*, Milan 1892.
   Baraonda, Milan 1894.
   Romanticismo, Milan 1900. 65, 67.
Marco Praga, *La Crisi*, Milan 1905. 65, 67.
Roberto Bracco, *Teatro*, Milan, Palermo, Naples s. a.   67.
Giacinto Callina, *Serenìssima*, Milan 1889. 67.
Ruggero Bonghi, *Leone XIII e il governo italiano*, Rome 1882.

Ruggero Bonghi, *Stòria di Roma*, Milan 1884-96.   **68.**
Alessandro Chiappelli, *Studi di antica letteratura cristiana*, Florence 1887. **68.**
Gaetano Negri, *Rumori mondani*, Milan 1889.
  L'Imperatore Giuliano, Milan 1902.
  Giòrgio Eliot, Milan 1903.   **68.**
Alfredo Oriani, *La lotta polìtica in Itàlia*, Florence 1917.
  Fino a Dògali, Bari 1918.   **68.**
Alessandro d'Àncona, *Orìgini del teatro italiano*, Florence-Rome 1891.
  La poesia popolare italiana, Leghorn 1878.   **68.**
Adolfo Bartoli, *I Precursori del Boccàccio e alcune delle sue fonti*, Florence 1876.   **68.**
Francesco d'Ovidio, *Studi sulla Divina Commèdia*, Milan-Palermo 1901.   **68.**
Pasquale Villari, *La Stòria di Geròlamo Savonarola e de' suoi tempi*, Florence 1898.   **68.**
Benedetto Croce, *Estètica*, Bari 1913.
  Saggi sulla letteratura italiana del seicento, Bari 1910.
  La letteratura della nuova Itàlia, Bari 1914-15.   **69.**
Giovanni Gentile, *Guerra e fede*, Naples 1918.   **70.**
Alfredo Panzini, *La lanterna di Diògene*, Milan 1907.
  Pìccole stòrie di un mondo grande, Milan 1906.
  Novelle d'ambo i sessi, Milan s. a. (1918).
  Viàggio di un pòvero letterato, Milan 1919.   **70.**
Enrico Corradini, *La Pàtria lontana*, Milan 1910.
  La Guerra lontana, Milan 1911.   **70.**
Vilfredo Pareto, *Trattato di sociologia generale*, Florence 1917.
  I sistemi socialisti.   BE.   **70.**
F. T. Marinetti, *Manifesti del futurismo*.   BE.   **71.**
Giuseppe Prezzolini, *Dopo Caporetto*, Florence 1919.
  Vittòrio Veneto, Florence 1919.   **72.**
Giovanni Papini, *Un Uomo finito*, Florence 1918.
  Giorni di festa, Florence 1919.
  24 cervelli, Milan 1918.
  Testimonianze, Milan 1919.
  Stroncature, Florence 1918.   **72.**
Èrcole Luigi Morselli, *Stòrie da ridere . . . e da piàngere*, Milan 1918.
  Orione. Glàuco. Milan 1919.   **72.**
Ardengo Sòffici, *Giornale di bordo*, Florence 1918.
  Kòbilek, Florence 1918.   **72.**

Index of Authors

Accolti, Bernardo (d. 1534), 21.
Alamanni, Luigi (1495-1556), 24.
Alberti, Leòn Battista (1407-72), 28.
Aleardi, Aleardo (1812-96), 59.
Alfieri, Vittòrio (1749-1803), 41, 42, 43, 46, 47, 49, 61.
Algarotti, Francesco (1712-64), 40.
Alighieri, Dante (1265-1321), 10, 11, 13, 14, 40, 43.
Amari, Michele (1806-89), 56.
Ambrogini, Àngelo (Poliziano) (1454-94), 19, 20, 26, 27.
Andreini, Giovanni Battista (1578-1652), 35.
Angiolieri, Cecco (?-1312), 11.
Antona-Traversi, Giannino, 67.
Aquilano, Serafino, see Ciminelli.
Aretino, Pietro (1492-1556), 23, 27, 28.
Arienti, Giovanni Sabbadino degli (d. 1510), 26.
Ariosto, Lodovico (1474-1533), 23, 26, 28, 29, 31, 35.
Assisi, S. Francesco d' (1182-1226), 8.

Balbo, Cèsare (1789-1853), 56.
Bandello, Matteo (1480?-1565), 26, 35.
Baretti, Giuseppe (1719-89), 43, 44, 49.
Barrili, Antòn Giùlio (1836-88), 65.
Bàrtoli, Adolfo (1833-94), 68.
Bàrtoli, Daniello (1608-85), 36.
Bartolomeo da S. Concòrdio, see S. Concòrdio.
Barzizza, Gasparino (1395-1431), 19.

Beccari, Agostino (wrote 1554), 27.
Beccari, Antonio (da Ferrara) (1315-63?), 15.
Beccaria, Cèsare (1738-94), 40, 44.
Belli, Giuseppe Gioachino (1791-1863), 55.
Bembo, Pietro (1470-1547), 21.
Beolco, Àngelo (Ruzzante), 27.
Berchet, Giovanni (1783-1851), 50, 51, 54.
Berni, Francesco (1497-1535), 28.
Bettinelli, Savèrio (1718-1808), 40.
Biondo, Flàvio (da Forlì) (1388-1463), 19.
Boccàccio, Giovanni (1313-75), 12, 14, 26, 27.
Boccalini, Traiano (1556-1613), 36.
Boiardo, Matteo Maria (1440-94), 21, 22, 23, 26.
Bòito, Arrigo (1842-1918), 60.
Bonghi, Ruggero (1826-95), 68.
Bònichi, Bindo (d. 1338), 15.
Botero, Giovanni (1540-1617), 36.
Botta, Carlo (1766-1835), 48.
Bracciolini, Francesco (1566-1645), 34.
Bracciolini, Pòggio (1380-1459), 19.
Bracco, Roberto (b. 1861), 67.
Bruni, Leonardo (Aretino) (1370-1444), 19.
Bruno, Giordano (1548-1600), 27, 32, 33, 35.
Buonarroti, Michelàngelo (1475-1564), 22, 25, 31, 32.

Burchiello (Domènico di Giovanni) (1404–49), 20.
Butti, Enrico Annìbale (1865–1911), 60.

Campanella, Tommaso (1568–1639), 36.
Cantù, Cèsare (1804–95), 55.
Càrcano, Giùlio (1812–84), 55.
Carducci, Giosuè (1835–1907), 60, 62, 63, 68.
Cariteo, *see* Gareth, Benedetto.
Caro, Annìbale (1507–66), 27, 28.
Castelvetro, Lodovico (1505 ?–71), 28.
Casti, Giovanni Battista (1724–1803), 44.
Castiglione, Baldesàr (1478–1529), 29.
Cattàneo, Carlo (1801-69), 56.
Cavalca, Domenico, 11.
Cavalcanti, Guido (1259 ?–1300), 9, 10.
Cavour, Camillo Benso di (1810–61), 57, 58.
Cecchi, Giovanni Maria (1518–87), 27.
Cellini, Benvenuto (1500–71), 29.
Cèsari, Antònio (1760–1828), 47.
Cesarotti, Michele (1730–1808), 39.
Chiabrera, Gabriello (1552–1638), 34.
Chiappelli, Alessandro (b. 1857), 68.
Chiari, Pietro (1711–85), 43.
Ciminelli, Serafino (Aquilano) (1466–1500), 21.
Cino da Pistòia, *see* Sigisbuldi.
Collettà, Pietro (1775–1831), 48, 55.
Colonna, Vittòria (1492–1547), 21, 22.
Compagni, Dino (1257 ?–1324), 11.
Conti, Antònio (1677–1749), 37, 38, 39.

Conti di antichi cavalieri, 10.
Corradini, Enrico (b. 1868), 70.
Cossa, Pietro (1830–81), 62.
Costanzo, Àngelo, *see* di Costanzo, A.
Croce, Benedetto (b. 1866), 69, 70, 71.
Cuoco, Vincenzo (1770–1823), 48.

da Filicàia, Vincenzo (1642–1707), 34.
Dàlcamo, Cielo (first half of thirteenth cent.), 8.
dall' Òngaro, Francesco (1810–73), 60.
d'Ambra, Francesco (1499–1558), 27.
d'Ancona, Alessandro (1835–1914), 68.
d'Annùnzio, Gabriele (b. 1864), 63, 64, 65, 66, 67, 70, 71.
Dante, *see* Alighieri.
da Porto, Luigi (1485–1529), 26.
d'Aragona, Tùllia (1506–56 ?), 21.
Dàvila, Enrico Caterino (1576–1631), 36.
d'Azèglio, Màssimo Taparelli (1798–1866), 52, 55.
de Amicis, Edmondo (1846–1908), 65.
Deledda, Gràzia (b. 1875), 65.
della Casa, Giovanni (1503–56), 29.
dell' Anguillàia, Ciacco (thirteenth cent.), 11.
de Marchi, Emìlio (1851–1910), 64.
de Sanctis, Francesco (1818-83), 62, 69.
di Costanzo, Àngelo (1507–84 ?), 21.
di Giàcomo, Salvatore (b. 1860), 64.
di Tàrsia, Galeazzo (d. 1533), 21.
Doni, Antòn Francesco (1513–74), 26.

d'Ovìdio, Francesco (b. 1847), 68.
Dovizi, Bernardo (da Bibbiena) (1470-1520), 26.
Duprè, Giovanni (1817-82), 55.

Erizzo, Sebastiano (1525-85), 26.

Farina, Salvatore (b. 1846), 65.
Ferrara, Antònio da, see Beccari, Antònio.
Ferrari, Giuseppe (1811-76), 56.
Ferrari, Pàolo (1822-89), 62.
Ferrari, Severino (1856-1905), 61.
Ficino, Marsìlio (1433-99), 20.
Filangieri, Gaetano (1752-88), 44.
Filelfo, Francesco (1398-1481), 19.
Filicàia, Vincenzo da, see da Filicàia.
Fiorentino, ser Giovanni (wrote 1378), 15.
Fioretti di S. Francesco, 11.
Firenzuola, Àgnolo (1493-1546?), 26.
Fogazzaro, Antònio (1842-1911), 60, 64, 66, 67.
Folengo, Teòfilo (Merlìn Cocai; Limerno Pitocco) (1496-1544), 23.
Fortini, Pietro (1500?-62), 26.
Fòscolo, Ugo Niccolò (1778-1827), 46, 47, 49, 50, 61.
Francesco da Barberino (1264-1348), 11.
Francesco di V., see Vannozzo.
Franco, Niccolò (1515-70), 28.
Franco, Verònica (1546-91), 21.
Frederick II (Hohenstaufen) (1194-1250), 8, 9.
Frenzi, Giùlio de' (Luigi Federzoni), 70.
Frescobaldi, Dino (d. 1320), 10.
Frescobaldi, Matteo (d. 1348), 14.
Frezzi, Federico (135-?-1417), 14.
Frugoni, Carlo Innocenzo (1692-1768), 37.

Fucini, Renato (b. 1843), 64.
Fusinato, Arnaldo (1817-88), 54.

Galeani, Napione Gianfrancesco (1748-1830), 47.
Galiani, Ferdinando (1728-87), 38, 40.
Galilei, Galileo (1564-1642), 36, 44.
Gallina, Giacinto (1852-91), 67.
Galluppi, Pasquale (1770-1846), 56.
Gàmbara, Verònica (1485-1550), 21.
Gareth, Benedetto (Cariteo) (1450?-1514), 21.
Gazzoletti, Antònio (1813-66), 55.
Genovesi, Antònio (1712-69), 44.
Gentile, Giovanni, 70.
Giacometti, Pàolo (1817-82), 62.
Giacosa, Giuseppe (1847-1906), 62, 67.
Gianni dei Ricevuti, Lapo (alive 1298, 1317), 10.
Giannone, Pietro (1676-1748), 44.
Giannone, Pietro (junior) (1792-1872), 54.
Gioberti, Vincenzo (1801-52), 56, 57, 70.
Giòia, Melchiorre (1767-1829), 50.
Giordani, Pietro (1774-1848), 48.
Giraldi, Giovanni Battista (1504-73), 26, 27.
Giusti, Giuseppe (1809-50), 53, 54.
Giustiniàn, Leonardo (1388?-1446), 20.
Goldoni, Carlo (1707-93), 27, 42, 43, 49.
Gozzi, Carlo (1720-1806), 43.
Gozzi, Gàspare (1713-86), 44.
Graf, Arturo (1848-1913), 64, 68.
Grazzini, Antòn Francesco (il Lasca) (1503-84), 26, 27, 28.
Grossi, Tommaso (1791-1853), 52, 55.

Groto, Luigi (Cieco d'Àdia) (1541-85), 27.
Guadagnoli, Antònio (1798-1858), 54.
Guardati, Masùccio de' (Salernitano) (wrote 1476), 26.
Guarini, Giovanni Battista (1538-1612), 28.
Guarino da Verona (1374-1460), 19.
Guerrazzi, Domènico (1804-73), 52, 55.
Guerrini, Olindo (Lorenzo Stecchetti) (1845-1918), 61.
Guicciardini, Francesco (1483-1540), 29, 30.
Guidi, Alessandro (1650-1712), 34.
Guinizelli, Guido (c. 1230-c. 1275), 9, 10.

Jacopone da Todi (ser Jàcopo Benedetti) (1230?-1306), 8.

Landino, Cristòforo (1424-1504), 20.
Leonardo da Vinci (1452-1519), 31, 33.
Leopardi, Giàcomo (1798-1837), 52, 53, 54.
Lopez, Sabatino, 67.

Machiavelli, Niccolò (1469-1527), 17, 26, 29, 30, 31, 32, 33.
Maffei, Scipione (1675-1755), 37.
Mameli, Goffredo (1827-49), 54.
Manfredi, Eustàchio (1674-1734), 37.
Manzoni, Alessandro (1785-1873), 12, 47, 50, 51, 52, 64, 65.
Marenco, Leopoldo (1836-99), 62.
Marino, Giovanni Battista (1569-1625), 33, 34, 36.
Marradi, Giovanni (b. 1852), 61.

Martelli, Pièr Jàcopo (1665-1727), 37.
Masùccio, Salernitano, see Guardati.
Mazzini, Giuseppe (1805-72), 56, 70.
Mazzoni, Guido (b. 1859), 61.
Mèdici, Lorenzino de' (1514-48), 27.
Mèdici, Lorenzo de' (il Magnìfico) (1449-92), 20.
Menzini, Benedetto (1646-1704), 34, 35.
Metastàsio, Pietro (Pietro Trapassi) (1698-1782), 37, 38.
Michelàngelo, see Buonarroti.
Montemagno, Buonaccorso da (d. 1429), 14.
Monti, Vincenzo (1754-1828), 46, 47, 50.
Morselli, Luigi Èrcole (b. 1883), 72.
Muratori, Lodovico Antònio (1672-1750), 38, 44.

Negri, Ada (b. 1870), 64.
Negri, Gaetano (1838-1902), 68.
Nìccoli, Niccolò (1364-1437), 19.
Niccolini, Giovanni Battista (1782-1861), 52.
Nievo, Ippòlito (1831-61), 55.
Novellino, 10.

Oriani, Alfredo (1852-1909), 68, 70.

Pagano, Màrio (1748-99), 44.
Pallavicino, Sforza (1607-67), 36.
Pananti, Filippo (1760-1837), 54.
Panzini, Alfredo (b. 1863), 70.
Papini, Giovanni (b. 1881), 72.
Parabosco, Giròlamo (1524?-57), 26.
Parentucelli, Tommaso (Niccolò V) (1397-1445), 19.
Pareto, Vilfredo, 70.
Parini, Giuseppe (1729-99), 41, 43, 44, 45, 46, 47, 49, 61.

Paruta, Pàolo (1540-98), 35, 36.
Pascarella, Cèsare (b. 1858), 64.
Pàscoli, Giovanni (1855-1912), 63.
Paterno, Lodovico (wrote 1560), 28.
Pèllico, Sìlvio (1789-1854), 50, 51.
Perticari, Giùlio (1779-1822), 47.
Petrarca, Francesco (1304-74), 11, 12, 14, 17, 21.
Piccolòmini, Enea Sìlvio (Pius II) (1405-64), 19.
Pico della Miràndola, Giovanni (1463-94), 20.
Pindemonte, Ippòlito (1753-1828), 47.
Pistòia, see Cammelli.
Pizzicolli, Ciriaco de' (d'Ancona) (1391-1455), 19.
Poèrio, Alessandro (1802-48), 54.
Poliziano, see Ambrogini, Àngelo.
Pontano, Gioviano (1426-1503), 19.
Porta, Carlo (1776-1821), 55.
Praga, Emìlio (1839-75), 59.
Praga, Marco (b. 1862), 65, 67.
Prati, Giovanni (1814-84), 55, 59.
Prezzolini, Giuseppe, 72.
Pucci, Antònio (d. 1390), 15.
Pulci, Luigi (1432-84), 15, 22.

Quirini, Giovanni (d. 131-?), 14.

Rambaldoni, Vittorino (da Feltre) (1378-1446), 19.
Rapisardi, Màrio (1844-1912), 61.
Redi, Francesco (1626-98), 34.
Rinuccini, Cino (1350?-1417), 14.
Rolli, Pàolo (1687-1765), 37, 39.
Romagnosi, Giàn Domènico (1761-1835), 50.
Rosa, Salvatore (1615-73), 35.
Rosmini-Serbati, Antònio (1797-1855), 56

Rossetti, Gabriele (1783-1854), 54.
Rossi, Giovanni Gherardo de' (1754-1827), 41.
Rota, Bernardino (1506-75), 21.
Rovetta, Geròlamo (1851-1910), 65, 67.

Sacchetti, Franco (1330?-1400?), 15.
Salutati, Colùccio (Pièrio) (1331-1406), 76.
S. Concòrdio, Bartolomeo da (1262-1347), 11.
Sannazzaro, Jàcopo (1458-1530), 27.
Sarpi, Pàolo (1552-1623), 35.
Savioli, Lodovico (1729-1804), 41.
Savonarola, Giròlamo (1452-98), 25.
Serao, Matilde (b. 1856), 65.
Sercambi, Giovanni (1347-1424), 15.
Sergardi, Lodovico (1660-1726), 35.
Sermini, Gentile (wrote 1424), 26.
Sigisbuldi, Cino dei (da Pistòia) (1270?-1337?), 10.
Sòffici, Ardengo (b. 1883), 72.
Spedalieri, Nicola (1740-95), 44.
Speroni, Sperone (1500-88), 27.
Stampa, Gàspara (1523?-54), 21.
Stecchetti, Lorenzo, see Guerrini, Olindo.
Stigliani, Tommaso (1573-1651), 34.

Tansillo, Luigi (1510-68), 21, 24, 28.
Tàrsia, see di Tàrsia.
Tasso, Bernardo (1493-1569), 24.
Tasso, Torquato (1544-95), 21, 24, 25, 27, 28, 31.
Tassoni, Alessandro (1565-1635), 34, 35, 36.
Tebaldeo, Antònio (1463-1537), 21.

Tebaldi, Pieràccio (d. 1350?), 15.
Telèsio, Bernardino (1508?–88), 36.
Testi, Fùlvio (1593–1646), 34.
Tiraboschi, Geròlamo (1731–94), 44.
Tommaseo, Niccolò (1802–74), 59.
Traversari, Ambrògio (1386–1439), 19.
Trìssino, Giàn Giòrgio (1478–1550), 24, 27.

Uberti, Fàzio degli (130–?–68), 14.

Valla, Lorenzo (1405–57), 19, 68.
Vannozzo, Francesco di (wrote 1388), 16.

Vasari, Giòrgio (1511–74), 29.
Verga, Giovanni (b. 1840), 65.
Verri, Alessandro (1741–1816), 40.
Verri, Pietro (1738–94), 40, 44.
Vico, Giovanni Battista (1668–1744), 38, 39, 44, 68, 69.
Villani, Giovanni (128–?–1348), 11.
Villari, Pasquale (1827–1919), 68.
Vinciguerra, Antònio (d. 1502), 28.
Vittorelli, Jàcopo (1749–1835), 41.
Vittorino da Feltre, see Rambaldoni.

Zanella, Giàcomo (1820–88), 61.